The Story of the Blockchain

The Story of the Blockchain

A Beginner's Guide to the Technology That Nobody Understands

Omid Malekan

Triple Smoke Stack
NEW YORK

ISBN: 978-1-7320273-0-5 (paperback)
ISBN: 978-1-7320273-1-2 (e-book)

Cover design by Laura Duffy
Illustrations by Simon Sullivan
Book design by Karen Minster
Editor: Christina Verigan
Proofreader: Debra Nichols

PRINTED IN THE UNITED STATES OF AMERICA

Contents

Introduction

My initial foray into the world of blockchain technology and cryptocoins began, as it does for most people, in a state of confusion. It was early 2014, and the world's biggest Bitcoin exchange had just filed for bankruptcy after revealing that hackers had stolen most of its clients' coins.

To my former colleagues on Wall Street, most of whom had dismissed the very idea of Bitcoin from the outset, this was just further proof that digital money was inherently worthless.

I on the other hand was stuck on a more basic question: If bitcoins weren't worth anything, why would anyone go through the trouble of stealing them?

Eager to answer that question, I decided to get my hands on some and find out. A few hundred dollars deposited into a cryptocoin exchange later, I was the proud owner of a not-so-shiny bitcoin, and I was thoroughly unimpressed. That part of the experience was no different than buying shares of Apple through an online broker. Then I transferred my bitcoin from the exchange to my computer.

That was my *a-ha* moment.

Something about that transfer—a digital asset leaving the exchange and almost immediately arriving on my computer—challenged everything I knew and understood about economics and finance. The experience was totally alien, but also totally right, as if *this* was how money was meant to work.

And so, despite the fact that I wasn't sure what to do or how to do it, I dove right in. In the ensuing years, I bought, sold, transferred, mined, and lost countless different cryptocoins, making every possible mistake along the way. I read a bunch of technical manuals I didn't understand, interviewed people far smarter than I, and got used to feeling perplexed.

Things only began to make sense when I realized that understanding this world didn't come from studying complicated concepts, but from developing a new mindset, one not anchored to the old ways of doing things. That was also when I realized the true potential of this technology to improve our lives, beyond just money and banking.

This book is my attempt at passing that new mindset on to you. I'm not the most technically savvy person in this space, nor am I the most opinionated. But as fans of my prior work on YouTube and various other media outlets would probably tell you, I'm very good at explaining the seemingly unexplainable, by telling stories and using analogies from other walks of life.

Some of you will be disappointed to learn that this is not an investment book, and that I have no idea whether you should invest in cryptocoins. There are other books on that subject out there, but I couldn't recommend any of them, as I concluded long ago that the people who know how to make money investing are too busy doing so to write investment books.

Instead, what I offer you here is something potentially more valuable: a basic understanding of a technology that will eventually impact everything, but which, at the moment, few people understand.

Most of the other educational materials in this field focus on the *how*, talking about complex subjects like cryptography and game theory. Those concepts are important, as we'll see later in the book, but my primary goal here is to convince you of the *why*. At its core, the story of the blockchain is a story about trust: where it comes from, why we need it, and how a collection of ideas and technologies are coming together to radically alter the ways in which we can trust each other.

To help you along as you read this story, I've included a simple glossary of nontechnical definitions, along with a tutorial on how to get started by safely making your first crypto-coin transactions.

But for now, I'd like to begin this story by taking you back to the turn of the millennium and discussing what happened to the music business.

1

Blockchain

Nineteen ninety-nine was a pivotal year for the music business. Record companies celebrated a new all-time high in profitability, thanks to growing sales of the lucrative compact disc format. They were oblivious to the fact that CDs would soon be rendered obsolete, because 1999 was also the year the Napster file-sharing service launched, ushering in the digital music era. That one piece of software ended up sealing the fate of an entire industry.

Before the digital age, the only way for consumers to purchase music was by buying a physical device, whether it was a vinyl record, cassette tape, or CD. Although the underlying technology improved somewhat over the years, the limitations stayed the same. To own the music, you had to go to a store and buy it. Even if you only wanted to listen to one song, you had to pay for an entire album. If you lost or damaged your cartridge, you had to buy another one. You could lend your album to a friend, but that would mean you couldn't listen to it anymore. These limitations are what made the recording industry profitable for most of its history.

Digital music first arrived on the scene in the form of mp3 files, and quickly obliterated all of those restrictions. Now you could download any song within seconds without having to visit a store, and enjoy listening to it on a myriad of devices wherever you happened to be. You could make as many backup copies as you wanted for free, and send a copy to a friend while still enjoying the music yourself. With the help of a file-sharing service like Napster, one person could share the same mp3 file with countless people all over the world.

The appeal to consumers was obvious: *Digital products are convenient.*

But for music sellers, that very convenience was the destruction of the industry as they knew it. Consumers could now buy individual songs, play a track a million times without wearing it out, and make unlimited copies to share with friends. The record labels made various attempts to disrupt the adoption of digital music, but they failed at every turn. Eventually, the traditional music industry came to its own conclusion: *Digital products are infinitely replicable, and therefore, worthless.*

These dual realizations have transformed and, in some ways, crippled multiple industries. From books to magazines to movies, the apparent trade-off between the conveniences of digital media and the business costs of replicability have seemed insurmountable—until now.

How Blockchain Redefines Ownership

The simplest definition of a **blockchain** is *a technology that allows for something digital to exist in only one place.* Imagine if you could download a music file and enjoy it with all of the conveniences of digital technology, but with one difference: The moment you sent it to your friend to listen to, you yourself no longer could.

The blockchain achieves this feat by combining multiple technologies, from cryptography to peer-to-peer networks (the same ones, ironically, that powered Napster), to form a decentralized and distributed public ledger of who owns, or has access to, something, at any given moment in time.

Figure 01. A Global Ledger

Let's say that you were the first person ever to purchase a digital music file from a record label via a blockchain. As soon as the transaction happened, a network of independent computers around the world would communicate with each other and write into the ledger that ownership of a file has been transferred from a record company to you. Let's also say that after you finished listening to the song, you decided to send it to a friend. After first confirming that you in fact own the file by checking the existing entries in the ledger, all of those computers would then agree on the transfer to your friend, and enter that exchange into the ledger as well.

A Chain of Owners

Follow this process across thousands or even millions of transactions, and you can see how the blockchain preserves the integrity of ownership. Everyone knows who owns what, because everyone can follow the existing ledger back to the beginning of time. There is no room for dispute. Whenever you receive something, the community has already made sure that the sender actually owns it, by looking at the path of how they acquired it.

In some ways, this process is similar to how your local municipality tracks the ownership of property, and has done so for centuries. By going to the local clerk's office, you can look up who owns a house you might be interested in buying. By looking at the chain of previous owners, you can make sure the current seller is the rightful titleholder. The blockchain digitizes this process while also improving it.

The clerk's office is a centralized store of information, and history has proven time and again that such places are fragile. If the office doesn't keep proper backups, vital information might be lost. If an employee makes a mistake in entering a transaction, it might go unnoticed. Worse yet, a malicious actor could bribe the office to change a record after the fact, or even submit forgeries to wrongly transfer a property to their name. The blockchain does away with these vulnerabilities.

Because the system is distributed, copies of the same chain are kept at thousands of independent locations around the world by different participants. Because it is decentralized, it cannot easily be penetrated or changed by any one bad actor. Since nobody owns the blockchain, it is almost impossible to corrupt it in its entirety. This integrity is accomplished by the consensus mechanism, the process by which independent volunteers continuously come to agree on who owns something today and who should rightfully own it tomorrow.

Maintaining Integrity

In blockchain parlance, a **block** is a batch of transactions that get entered into the ledger at the same time. Entities that store previous blocks are called **nodes**; entities that write the newest block in the ledger are called **miners**. Both nodes and miners choose to be involved with the process for their own selfish purposes, either because they run a service that uses data from the ledger, or are being paid to maintain the network.

Miners are financially incentivized to maintain the integrity of the system. The particular incentive mechanism can vary depending on the blockchain, but the basic setup is always the same: The highest financial payouts go to the miners that write the truest ledgers.

One way this works is for a miner to charge each sender a tiny transaction fee for every file. The first such fee would be paid by the record company when it transfers a file to you.

Omid Malekan

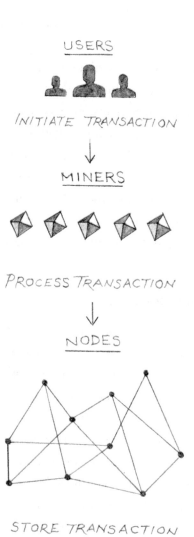

USERS

INITIATE TRANSACTION

↓

MINERS

PROCESS TRANSACTION

↓

NODES

STORE TRANSACTION

Figure 02.
From User to Miners to Nodes

Another fee would be paid if you decided to send the file to a friend. With each exchange, the miner that does the best and fastest job of writing an accurate entry in the ledger gets to keep the fee. The more honest a miner, the more money it makes. The entire process is guided by a clearly stated set of rules that everyone who decides to interact with that particular blockchain—be they a user, node, or miner—agrees to.

Few people might recognize it, but one of the greatest breakthroughs in the progress of human society was the invention of standardized accounting practices. Our economy is based on it. You agree to put your money in a bank because you understand that they will keep their books in a certain way. An investor is willing to buy shares in a company because it agrees to report its profits in a standard format, one used by other companies as well. This allows investors to make apples-to-apples comparisons of multiple organizations. Standardized accounting helps create trust where it wouldn't otherwise exist, and trust is the backbone of productive commerce.

The blockchain is the evolution of trust. It takes a previously agreed-upon way of accounting for ownership and applies the latest digital technology to make it work in real time. Because the ledger is distributed, decentralized, and transparent, all participants can trust that they will be treated fairly and honestly. And such treatment will last forever because, over the long term, everyone involved is financially incentivized to act fairly.

Just as accounting has a myriad of uses, so does the blockchain. The most obvious, easiest-to-implement, and, arguably, the most useful—is money.

CONSIDER THIS

- Profits from the sale of music in the United States reached a peak of $40 billion in 1999, then declined by over 60% in the next 15 years.

- At its peak, Napster had 80 million users, and accounted for more than half of all Internet traffic on some college campuses. It was ultimately forced to close by multiple copyright-infringement lawsuits from record labels and artists.

- Accounting as we know it today was invented by an Italian named Luca Pacioli who, in 1494, published a book describing the credit- and debit-based system of double-entry bookkeeping that is still widely used today.

2

Digital Money

The simplest definition of **money** is *a socially agreed upon store of value, unit of account, and means of exchange.* For thousands of years, human societies have found it helpful to make some sort of physical object their money. From seashells to shiny metal coins to green pieces of paper, money has often been something that has no intrinsic value. You can't eat your dollar bills or make a shelter with them but, because other people also ascribe to the same monetary convention, you can use your dollars to buy food and rent a house.

Over the years, money has evolved to offer better features. Metal coins are more durable than seashells, and paper bills are easier to carry around than gold ingots. When paper money became a preferred method of storage and exchange, banks rose up to facilitate the process, giving people a safe place to store their money, playing intermediary between borrowers and lenders, and helping facilitate large and long-distance transactions. As digital data storage and communication became the norm, banks adopted the technology to help speed up the movement of money but, despite appearances to the contrary, they've made surprisingly little progress.

How Money Moves

Fifty years ago, it took weeks to get a letter from someone in another country, a couple of days to get an international wire, and half an hour to drive to the record store and buy an LP. Today, streaming music and exchanging emails happen almost instantaneously. But receiving a wire transaction still takes as long as it used to, despite the fact that large banks are among the biggest spenders on information technology. It's not the *banks* that are outdated, but the money they exist to serve.

When someone wires you money, all that actually moves are a few bits of data. Your bank changes an entry in its computer that credits your account, and the sender's bank does the same in its computer to debit their account. Some sort of intermediary institution, like the Federal Reserve, then plays the same game of deduct here and add there between the two banks. In other words, you and the sender arrive at a *consensus* that their balance should go down and yours should go up. A series of intermediaries facilitates the process.

And so the same notion of consensus that rules a blockchain also rules our existing banking system. Since money has no intrinsic value, another way of looking at it is as *information*. The dollars in your wallet and the ones in your checking account are society's way of keeping track of your spending power—your place in the economy. Every time you buy something, your purchasing power declines while that of the seller increases. The idea of a consensus mechanism that tracks who has how much is as old as money itself, but until now, it has always been an intrinsic process, implied but not clearly spelled out.

The reason our current banking system is so outdated is because it's using a consensus mechanism invented for paper money and executing it digitally. It's no different than early versions of Internet encyclopedias, which took the text compiled for books and put it on their websites. This was an improvement over buying 32 volumes of the *Encyclopaedia Britannica*, but not nearly as powerful as Wikipedia, which uses its own consensus mechanism to continuously update in real time.

You can see this analogy play out in current forms of electronic payment. Services like Venmo and PayPal have the appearance of instant payments, but because they are built on top of an outdated banking model, transactions still take days to actually settle. In the meantime, what you see on their mobile apps when you check your balance is an IOU. This is why such services are never used for large transactions. The actual process of money moving around to resolve that IOU is painfully slow and woefully inefficient by modern standards, akin to an online encyclopedia updating its website only after it has shipped the latest print edition.

The Move to Digital Money on the Blockchain

Compared to a blockchain, our existing consensus mechanism of large financial institutions is not very good. It's more centralized, so it's more fragile. It offers little transparency and is far from immutable. Whereas blockchains continuously confirm the full integrity of the system with every transaction, in banking, issues of fraud and theft are often not discovered until long after the fact.

These flaws came to a head during the recent financial crisis, when investors and depositors woke up to a nightmare scenario of so-called too-big-to-fail banks that were seemingly incapable of properly accounting for their exposure to falling home prices. Given the rigid and centralized nature of the system, and the fact that just one bank failure could take the entire system down, governments around the world had no choice but to bail everyone out. It's no coincidence that the first blockchain was conceived during that period.

The nature of money is always evolving, and the change has always been preceded by technological improvement. Coins were not an option until mining and metallurgy allowed for mass production, and paper money didn't become an option until the invention of the printing press. Today, the growing ubiquity of computers and smartphones that are always connected to each other allows for the invention of a new kind of money, one that moves faster and more efficiently than anything we've ever seen before.

At first glance, replacing our existing system of paper money with something that only exists in cyberspace seems frightening, but the first forms of paper money were probably equally daunting. Society migrated to paper anyway, because the better features of a new kind of money proved irresistible.

Monetary evolution is usually slow, and has a lot of technological overlap. The first forms of paper money came into existence back when people used to leave their metal coins with goldsmiths for safe storage. In exchange, they would receive paper receipts that gave them the right to redeem their coins. Eventually people realized that using the paper receipts to do transactions was a lot easier than using the underlying coins— so much so that paper currency remained the most popular form of money long after it was no longer backed by gold.

Today the technology is being developed to allow people to transact their existing paper money over the blockchain, bypassing the inefficiencies of the banking system. As we all become more comfortable doing business that way, the door will be open to a new kind of currency that only exists in cyberspace. This new kind of money is called **cryptocurrency**, and the oldest one is Bitcoin.

CONSIDER THIS

o The ABA routing transit number, the nine-digit number used to identify a bank and printed at the bottom of every check, was first invented by the American Bankers Association over a century ago.

o International wire transactions are handled through the SWIFT network, a communication platform invented in the 1970s using the most cutting-edge technology of that era to allow banks to securely communicate funds transfers.

o In 1971, President Richard Nixon ended the U.S. government's program allowing dollars to be converted to gold. This ended the U.S. currency's last link to any kind of precious metal.

3

Bitcoin

The simplest definition of a cryptocoin is *a purely elec-tronic form of money designed to take advantage of the distributed, decentralized and trust-building nature of a blockchain.* The first-ever cryptocoin, **Bitcoin**, was invented in 2008 by an anonymous creator who went by the name of Satoshi Nakamoto. Others had tried to invent purely digital money before, but Nakamoto was the first to come up with a decentralized solution to the biggest challenge of money that only exists in cyberspace: the double-spend problem.

Physical money can only be spent once, for the obvious reason that once you give a coin to someone as payment, you no longer have it to give to someone else. However, with digital currency, spending the same money twice could be as easy as copying a file on a computer and sending it to multiple people. Early solutions to this fundamental problem relied on some sort of central authority to make sure the same money wasn't spent twice, somewhat defeating the point of digitizing money in the first place.

Nakamoto combined the latest developments in multiple areas of computer science to come up with a much more elegant solution: All Bitcoin transactions would have to be validated by a voluntary third party, one who would prove their intentions are honest by solving a complicated math puzzle first.

This is Bitcoin's **proof-of-work** mechanism, and what many consider to be Nakamoto's greatest contribution. The name comes from the fact that any miner hoping to write the latest transactions into the ledger must do work in the form of the hard-core computing required to solve the math puzzle. Solving that puzzle requires powerful computers, and running those computers requires a lot of electricity. In exchange for shelling out for those expenses up front, Bitcoin miners who succeed in solving the puzzle and writing the latest block are then rewarded with a payment, in bitcoins.

The more trustworthy the public considers the underlying infrastructure of a cryptocoin, the more valuable its coins. Since Bitcoin's miners get paid for their efforts in the very coin whose transactions they validate, their incentives are aligned with the users of the network—both want to maintain an accurate ledger. And so, a central authority is replaced by a network of volunteers pursuing their own financial self-interest.

The Upgraded Version of an Old Idea

Proof of work as a means of creating scarcity and value is an ancient concept. For as long as people have used physical forms of money, like shells and gold, putting work into the creation of that money, like making shell necklaces or gold coins, has made it more valuable. In that same spirit, a bitcoin that was transferred to you from someone else after having been put through hard-core computation is more valuable than something that can be sent as an email attachment.

A blockchain that uses proof of work to keep the writers of the latest transactions honest has many uses beyond crypto-coins. It can be used to track ownership and the transactions of any asset that could benefit from having a digital version, including electronic versions of existing money like dollars and euros. If Nakamoto had wanted to, he could have used his idea to improve the way in which we electronically transact existing forms of paper money and called it a day. But he was out to accomplish a lot more.

Scarcity Controlled by an Algorithm

One of the most significant attributes of paper money is the ability for the authorities to easily print more of it. Some people consider this a positive because the people in charge can vary the supply of money to deal with short-term emergencies like a financial crisis. But critics consider unconstrained supply a flaw because, as history teaches us, the temptation to print more is often hard to resist—and it usually ends badly.

Nakamoto designed Bitcoin so the maximum supply of coins that can ever exist is finite. In the beginning, the cryptocurrency began with only a few million coins in circulation. Although that number has risen over the years as miners are rewarded for their work with new coins, the number of new coins being created is steadily decreasing, and will eventually reach zero. This so-called **inflation schedule** is formulaic and is written into the software that rules every single Bitcoin transaction. The number of new coins that a miner gets paid for writing a new block gets cut in half every 210,000 blocks, and is set to go to zero after 64 such halvings. The formula allows us to estimate the number of coins outstanding to top out at around 21 million by the year 2140.

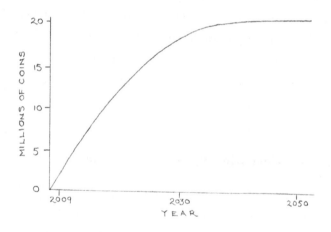

Figure 03. Bitcoin Inflation Schedule

To understand why someone would invent a coin with a fixed and predictable inflation schedule, it helps to look at the timing. Bitcoin was invented during the heart of the financial crisis, when our paper-based monetary system looked as if it were on the verge of collapse. The crisis was caused, in part, by many large financial institutions that had acted irresponsibly and borrowed too much. Instead of letting them suffer the consequences of their actions, the authorities decided to print historical amounts of money and bail them out.

When new money is printed, the value of all existing money goes down. To some, it seemed unfair that people who had acted responsibly and saved money were punished to bail out others who had not. It didn't help that the people in charge of our paper money system, the Treasury officials and central bankers of most countries, often had close personal ties to the failing banks they were bailing out. In other words, one of the worst fears of a centralized monetary system came true.

The Genesis Block

The first-ever Bitcoin transaction took place between Naka- moto and another developer in January of 2009. Along with the usual information about bitcoins changing ownership, that transaction also had a secret message embedded in it. It read:

TIMES 03/JAN/2009 CHANCELLOR ON BRINK
OF SECOND BAILOUT FOR BANKS.

This was a reference to a front-page story from the *Times of London* about how British authorities were preparing for another round of bailouts. Although the message was prob- ably included to prove the date of the first-ever transaction of the Bitcoin blockchain, it had the added benefit of reminding users that Bitcoin was a different kind of money—one not controlled by a government.

Most of the aforementioned features are unique to Bitcoin. Not every blockchain has to be used for a cryptocurrency, and not every cryptocurrency needs to have the same rules as Bitcoin. Since the invention of Bitcoin, other developers have introduced coins whose blockchains behave differently. Referred to collectively as **altcoins**, some have a tighter inflation schedule than Bitcoin, while others are more flexible. Some have tried to improve upon Bitcoin's proof-of-work mechanism or replace it with an entirely different way of keeping miners honest.

There are many different attributes to a cryptocoin and the blockchain on which it resides, and it's up to the community of developers and users of each unique currency to decide which features they want their money to have. One of the most varied attributes between chains is how they handle the dual mandate of being secure yet transparent, which is part of the ancient debate about what information should be public versus private.

CONSIDER THIS

o If Satoshi Nakamoto were to publicly step forward today, he would mostly likely be a billionaire, as there are multiple Bitcoin accounts associated with him that contain vast amounts of coins.

o Over the years multiple media reports have claimed to reveal Nakamoto's identity, but none have panned out. In the spring of 2016, an Australian programmer and hacker publicly "outed" himself as the Bitcoin inventor. He managed to win over some of the cryptocoin's most prominent developers, but most of the proof he gave was eventually discredited by the community.

o The amount of electricity needed to mine bitcoins is not trivial, by design. Estimates of its blockchain's total energy usage vary, but most experts agree that it is now more than the daily power consumption of a small country.

o Although the fall of the Roman Empire is attributed to multiple causes, the debasement of its currency clearly played a part.

o Since the start of the financial crisis, central banks around the world have printed $10 trillion worth of additional paper money.

4

Public and Private

In designing Bitcoin to be fully decentralized with no governing body, Satoshi Nakamoto understood that he was asking users to take a leap of faith. Switching from a system of money controlled by governments to one ruled by mathematics and code is frightening. To help bridge the gap, he proposed full transparency.

Every Bitcoin transaction since the very first one is public for everyone to see. You can download the entire history of the cryptocoin onto your personal computer, or look up the current balance of any account by visiting a website like the one shown in Figure 04.

All of this was designed to make you comfortable that the network has integrity, and that every coin on the network resides in the account of its rightful owner. The only thing you can't look up is who that owner is.

Public Yet Anonymous

In Bitcoin, accounts are referred to as **addresses**, and are represented by a random string of letters and numbers. There are no names, email addresses, or Social Security numbers associated with them. To access the coins in an address, a

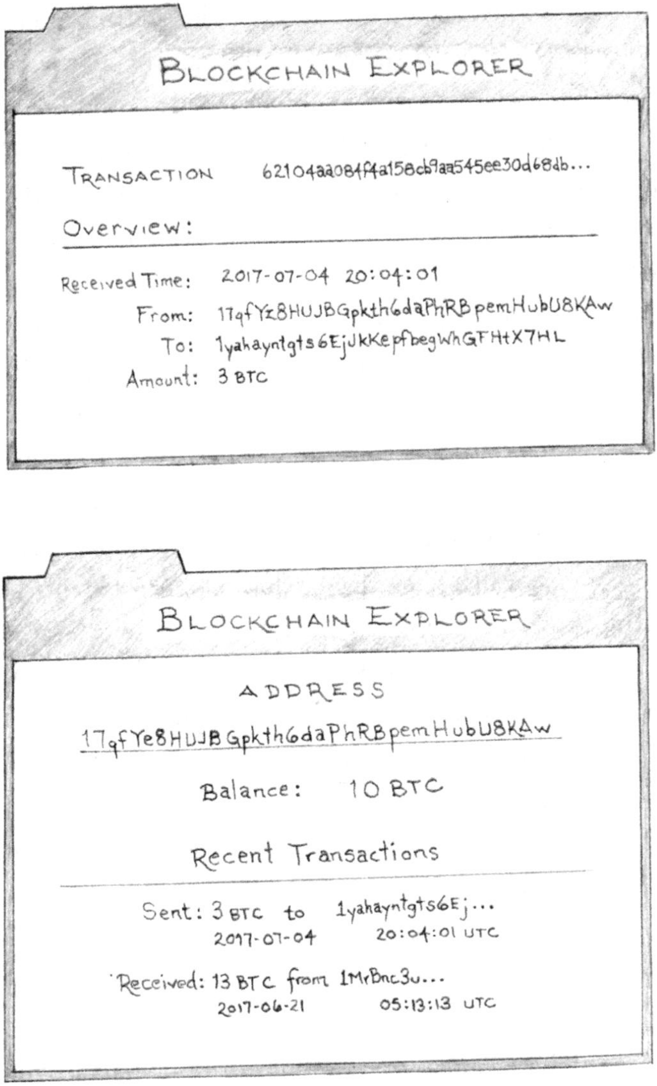

BLOCKCHAIN EXPLORER

TRANSACTION   62104aa084f4a158cb9aa545ee30d68db...

Overview:

Received Time: 2017-07-04 20:04:01
        From: 17qfYz8HUJBGpkth6daPhRBpemHubU8KAw
          To: 1yahayntgts6EjukKepfbegWhGFHtX7HL
      Amount: 3 BTC

BLOCKCHAIN EXPLORER

ADDRESS

17qfYe8HUJBGpkth6daPhRBpemHubU8KAw

Balance: 10 BTC

Recent Transactions

Sent: 3 BTC to   1yahayntgts6Ej...
        2017-07-04   20:04:01 UTC

Received: 13 BTC from 1MrBnc3u...
        2017-06-21   05:13:13 UTC

Figure 04.
Exploring the Blockchain on a Website

user needs to possess a second string of letters and numbers, known as the **private key**. The public address is what you share with anyone you wish to do a transaction with. But your private key is something you keep secret, because anyone that has it can access your money. In practice, this combination is not that different from having a public email address with a secret password.

But because Bitcoin is decentralized, there is no central authority that rules who is the rightful owner of any address, or the coins inside of it. Whereas in traditional banking an institution ties every account to an individual, the Bitcoin blockchain only ties each address to a private key. Storing bitcoins on the blockchain then is no different than storing physical money in a safe. Anyone that gets their hands on the combination can take what's inside—and there is no way to get your money back or punish the thief.

This public/private hybrid is both the appeal and the danger of using bitcoins as money. On the one hand, the transparency of the ledger gives you confidence that every transaction is legitimate, and the fact that only you and your counterpart know who you are gives you the privacy to do whatever you want. On the other hand, you and only you are responsible for keeping your money secure. There is no fraud department to call when something goes wrong.

Not all blockchains, or electronic forms of money built on a blockchain, need to have these specific attributes. There are blockchains that give each participant a unique identifier, one that can easily be tied to a name or Social Security number.

There are also cryptocoins that offer even more anonymity than Bitcoin.

Variety of Anonymity

Although Bitcoin transactions are anonymous to outsiders, every time one party does a transaction with another, both become somewhat exposed. Once you know your counterparty's Bitcoin address, you can easily look up their balance and transaction history, giving you access to information they might prefer to keep private.

Other cryptocurrencies have been invented to eliminate this possibility by offering their users even more privacy. These coins, with names like Monero and Zcash, still utilize a decentralized and distributed blockchain to handle all transactions, and some version of proof of work to keep their miners honest.

But they also put each transaction into a sort of digital blender before entering it into the ledger, mixing up attributes like the amount being transacted. This way, even if you have someone's public address, you can't automatically figure out much about them by surfing the blockchain's history, other than the fact that your transaction with them took place and was validated by the network. If you want to learn more, they have to give you permission, via a secondary mechanism.

Some users will be drawn to these other coins, while others will prefer the simplicity and greater transparency of

Bitcoin. Like any other technology that allows for privacy and anonymity, cryptocoins will also appeal to criminals and subversives. The same features that will allow opposition parties to raise funds to protest dictatorships will also allow tax evaders to hide their income.

The trade-offs between transparency and anonymity exist on a spectrum, and it will be up to each individual user, as well as our society as whole, to decide where on that spectrum they would like their money to be. Thankfully, it is easy to make an informed decision about a blockchain's attributes. Almost everything in the cryptocurrency space is **open-source**, meaning that anyone can peek under the hood to see how the underlying software works. Just as the verification of each transaction is distributed, so is the verification that a cryptocurrency's features work as advertised.

This radical culture of transparent rules executed by volunteers on a decentralized blockchain has the potential to improve more areas of life than just money. It can also improve the nature of computing itself.

CONSIDER THIS

- The current size of the Bitcoin blockchain is approximately 160 gigabytes, meaning you can download the history of every transaction to most basic computers.

o Since everything on the blockchain is transparent, you can start by looking up the first-ever transaction and walking your way forward. Just enter transaction ID 4a5e1e4baab89f3a32518a88c31bc87f618f76673e2cc77ab2127b7afdeda33b into a website like blockchain.info.

o Every bitcoin in existence today can be traced back to one of two sources: It was either part of the original bunch created by Satoshi Nakamoto to test out his idea, or it is a new coin created by the mining algorithm to pay a miner.

o Cryptocurrencies that offer additional privacy features are popular in dark-web markets where illicit materials are sold.

5

Ethereum

I n late 2013, a young developer named Vitalik Buterin published a white paper titled "A Next-Generation Smart Contract and Decentralized Application Platform." He began by praising the technological breakthroughs of Bitcoin, then proposed a series of additional features that would allow a similar blockchain to do much more. Less than two years later, the Ethereum blockchain platform was born.

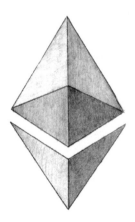

Figure 05. Ethereum logo

At base level, Ethereum is similar to Bitcoin. It uses a decentralized and distributed ledger to track the transactions of its own cryptocoin, called *ether*. Thousands of independent machines called nodes maintain copies of every transaction going back to the beginning of the blockchain, and independent miners participate in a proof-of-work mechanism that pays them to do complex computational work to process the latest changes. But in a key departure from Bitcoin, the Ethereum blockchain can also execute programming instructions.

Buterin chose the name for his project as a reference to ether, the transparent substance that was once believed to fill the universe and serve as the medium through which light traveled. Ethereum, on account of its ability to execute computer code on a blockchain, is like a giant computer that everyone gets to use simultaneously.

The World Computer

Programs running on Ethereum are in some ways no different than programs that run on your smartphone. They are a collection of variables and algorithms that, when executed by a machine, give a predictable outcome. But there is a key difference. An app on your smartphone is a slave to the single device it's running on. Conversely, programs on Ethereum run on thousands of machines—the nodes of the blockchain—at the same time.

Redundancy is an important requirement for computer systems that must always be running. Take, for example, an air-traffic control system that can't ever be down because thousands of planes in the air continuously await its instructions. Until now, the only way to obtain such redundancy was to either invest in tons of hardware yourself or pay a third party to access their cloud-computing network. One solution is expensive, and the other requires you to sacrifice privacy and autonomy. The blockchain offers a third way.

Just as a decentralized and distributed network that nobody owns increases the reliability of electronic money, it also improves the reliability of software, especially in situations where two parties who need to interact don't trust each other.

Ethereum comes with its own sophisticated programming language. This means users can ask the blockchain to not only move money, but also to run complex computer code, the kind needed to automate everything from complex financial transactions to a public bike-share program.

Software You Can Trust

To facilitate this, Ethereum allows for different programs written to the blockchain to reference *each other*. This allows for the creation of sophisticated programs that are open to the public, referred to as decentralized applications, or *dapps*. The simplest definition of a **dapp** is an *open-source and distributed program residing on a blockchain that performs a specific function.*

Dapps are the natural evolution of software in the age of the web. To understand why, it helps to study the evolution of the traditional encyclopedia. In the beginning, publishers, a kind of central authority, would collect information and distribute it to individuals who would buy their books. The advent of the web allowed them to make the information available to more readers, but trust was still placed in a single source, like the *Encyclopaedia Britannica*.

Wikipedia revolutionized this process. Instead of relying on a small group of experts to furnish its content, it opened things up to the public, offering them an organized and decentralized platform to facilitate reaching a consensus. What gives users comfort in using Wikipedia is not the authority of any particular contributor, but rather the way the system provides references and tracks every change. Trust now comes from a process.

Dapps on Ethereum do the same for software.

Most of the software we use today is written by large organizations who intentionally mask what's underneath the hood and ask users to trust them based on their reputation. Dapps running on the Ethereum platform on the other hand, by virtue of being executed by the blockchain, are **open-source**, meaning anyone can look up how they operate. Both the process of writing software and using it is democratized. Anyone can write a dapp, which everyone else can inspect before choosing to use, gaining trust from the process.

This evolution comes with a few trade-offs. Dapps tend to be slow compared to traditional software because they must constantly wait for all the nodes that maintain the blockchain to implement them. They also require learning a new kind of computer programming, because running a dapp is not free.

Since dapps shift the work of executing a program from local computers to the miners of the blockchain, and the miners have to be compensated for their work, each Ethereum dapp has to literally pay the network to run it. In the parlance of Ethereum, this payment is called **gas**, but is simply additional ether provided by the user as compensation to the miners maintaining the network. Instead of traditional software like Microsoft Office, where you pay just once (or a monthly fee) in exchange for using it as often as you like, dapps on Ethereum charge you *per use*, with the cost being tied to how complicated the computation needed to execute that decentralized application is.

Any kind of software can theoretically be turned into a dapp run on Ethereum. The more important trust and reliability are to the user, the greater the appeal of moving it onto the blockchain-based platform. Programs that also move around money would benefit even more, given the platform's built-in ability to move around its cryptocoin, ether. If the creators of a dapp would rather not use ether as their program's base currency, they also have the option of creating something called a token.

CONSIDER THIS

o Vitalik Buterin was only 19 years old when he published the Ethereum white paper, and he still remains the head of the organization that leads the project.

Many in the blockchain community consider him a savant.

o Although Ethereum is one of the younger blockchain projects out there, it has consistently been the second or third biggest in value.

o Other than the ability to process programming instructions, Ethereum differs from Bitcoin in other areas as well, including a more relaxed inflation schedule.

o The first dapp to go viral on Ethereum was a game called CryptoKitties. It allows users to buy, collect, and breed digital cats, with the integrity of ownership of each cat being preserved by the blockchain.

6

Tokens

M ost blockchain enthusiasts have a special fondness for Bitcoin, as it's the most popular digital money and the first-ever cryptocoin. But technically speaking, Bitcoin is nothing more than a dapp, as it is only decentralized code that runs on a blockchain and gains our trust by having clearly defined rules that govern its existence.

Once a blockchain that can process programming instructions is built, it's easy to create a new cryptocoin, or as many as a person would like. All it takes is coming up with some parameters and feeding them to the network. Since Ethereum is an ideal platform for doing just that, its creators went ahead and made the process of creating new cryptocurrencies even easier.

DIY Cryptocoins

New cryptocurrencies created on Ethereum are called **tokens**, and they behave the same way as the blockchain's native currency, ether. Users can send and receive tokens just as they do ether. Every address on Ethereum can hold not just ether, but also an infinite variety of tokens, each of which can be accessed by anyone that owns the private key to that address.

ETHEREUM BLOCKCHAIN EXPLORER

ADDRESS

0xfB6916095ca1df60bB79Ce92cE3Ea74c37c5d359

Overview:

ETH Balance: 25 ETH
Token Balance:
        EOS: 80
        OMG: 200
        STORJ: 1250

Figure 06.
An Ethereum Address Holding Tokens

New tokens are created by writing and uploading code that defines the rules to their existence.

Tokens have quickly become one of the most popular aspects of Ethereum. Since the main purpose of a blockchain is to offer a better way of tracking ownership, combining the convenience of digital with the trustworthiness of physical, a token can be used to represent any asset for which keeping track of ownership might be important.

Stocks, bonds, digital media, concert tickets, gift cards, frequent flyer miles, real estate, collectibles, gold, dollars, and countless other things qualify for tokenization. In some instances, like with frequent flyer miles, a token might represent ownership of something that exists only in the abstract. In others, tokens can track the ownership of a physical entity, like the deed to a house. To the blockchain, every token is just a few bits of data that is attached to a specific address. What that data pertains to is up to the creators of each token to decide and program into the blockchain.

Solving Real-World Problems

Let's say that you are the organizer of a concert and want to sell 100 tickets to a show. You also don't mind if the original buyers of the tickets sell them to others. Under our current system, you have to involve the services of a middleman like StubHub to create a secondary market for your tickets and make sure that nobody is selling counterfeits or selling the same ticket twice. Such middlemen are expensive.

There is a much more elegant solution to this problem using tokens on Ethereum. All you'd have to do is create a token called ConcertTicket and sell 100 of them. Each token could be exchanged for an actual ticket on the day of the event, but in the meantime, they could be freely traded via the Ethereum blockchain. Now, instead of buyers and sellers in the secondary market having to rely on an intermediary to confirm ownership, they could rely on the distributed ledger of the blockchain, gaining more trust while paying a fraction of the fees.

This is only one possible use for a token; there are countless more. A retailer might decide to issue gift cards as tokens to more efficiently track their ownership and usage. An inventor might raise funds by issuing tokens that can then be redeemed for her invention. A borrower might give his lenders tokens with an added feature of paying out interest to whoever happens to own the token come payment time. An online casino might use tokens instead of chips. A video-game maker might use tokens as the in-game currency. A charity might issue every donor a token that has the added feature of allowing them to vote on how funds should be spent. A content company might issue tokens that represent the rights to reproduce creative content like songs. A startup might issue tokens to investors instead of going public and issuing shares.

All of these already exist as active tokens on Ethereum, and there are thousands more. Any human activity that involves multiple users, is defined by a transparent set of rules, and requires trust to prosper is a candidate to be tokenized and run on Ethereum. The main role that the blockchain plays in such endeavors is to remove inefficient and slow intermediaries like banks, exchanges, crowdfunding sites, and secondary markets.

Tokens, along with dapps, are two key features of any blockchain that can handle programming instructions, such as Ethereum. A third feature is the ability to create an automated agreement between two parties, the terms of which are enforced by the blockchain. Such agreements are technically referred to as smart contracts.

CONSIDER THIS

○ There are currently over 40,000 different tokens on Ethereum, and new ones are created every single day.

○ The most valuable token is EOS, which is, ironically, the funding currency for one of Ethereum's competitors.

○ Many startups in the blockchain space fund themselves with a crowdsale, issueing tokens to their contributors in exchange for cryptocoins sent via the blockchain.

7

Smart Contracts

One of the more striking attributes of a well-thought-out blockchain is its inherent sense of fairness. Since the nodes and miners that preserve the network only see numbers, all participants are treated equally. Since every transaction is processed using a preestablished and transparent set of rules, everyone knows what to expect. Since no corporation owns it, and no government can control it, the system cannot easily be corrupted. The blockchain is the technological embodiment of lady justice, blind to prejudice and treating everyone the same.

Such a platform is perfect for inventing a new kind of money like Bitcoin, or running software more reliably as on Ethereum, but can also revolutionize other forms of human interaction, like contracts.

Contracts play a central role in practically everything we do. From the lease on an apartment to the terms of an insurance policy, almost all forms of commerce that involve a substantial payment are ruled by a contract. Under our present system, a contract is written before the transaction, but is only enforceable *after the fact*. If someone violates the terms of an agreement, you take them to court and ask a third party to intervene on your behalf.

This system works, more or less, but can be complicated, slow, expensive, and inefficient. There are people who thrive on exploiting its loopholes, and it requires middlemen such as attorneys to function. It also has a historical tendency to discriminate against the poor and powerless.

Upgraded and Automated

A blockchain turns our current system of contract enforcement upside down. Because it's blind, it cannot discriminate in favor of some members over others. Because it's entirely rule based, there is no need for interpretation, and no room for manipulation. Because it's always running, judgments are handed out *in real time.*

The simplest definition of a **smart contract** is *an agreement between different parties, executed in real time on a blockchain, in a manner that is guaranteed to satisfy all those who agreed to its terms.*

Smart contracts replace the complicated legal-language of ordinary contracts, along with their propensity for loopholes and need for interpretation, with the simple rule-based language of computers. The most basic smart contracts hold digital money in escrow until a certain condition is satisfied, then automatically pay the rightful recipient.

That idea in and of itself is not that revolutionary, and not so different from using your bank's bill-pay feature to sign up for automatic payment of your electric bill. What is revolutionary is the ability to guarantee that such a transaction always goes through flawlessly, thanks to the impartiality and reliability of the blockchain.

In our current setup, it's not always obvious who is at fault if a scheduled payment doesn't reach its destination, so the legal system spends tremendous resources trying to get to the bottom of that very question. But on the blockchain, ascribing fault is as easy as inspecting the underlying code of the smart contract. Better yet, so long as the code is written properly in the first place, in a manner all parties agree to, such a mistake can never happen. Blockchains replace the code of law with the law of code.

There are many profound implications to this new way of managing contracts. Any agreement that involves money changing hands based on a fixed set of rules is a candidate to become a smart contract, eliminating layers of uncertainty, middlemen, and expense along the way.

Take the example of a simple bet on a football game. Imagine the two parties involved don't trust each other. Under the current system, they have to seek out a middleman, like a casino, and give it their money to hold, along with instructions to pay the winner based on the outcome of the game. The casino charges a fee for this service, and introduces the additional risk of the third party making a mistake or being corrupted.

This same bet can easily be executed on a blockchain designed to handle programming instructions. Code that lays out the terms of the bet in a manner that both parties agree to is uploaded to the blockchain as a smart contract, and each bettor sends his or her wager to that contract to hold. Once the game is finished, the contract references an official source like the NFL website to determine who won, then pays the rightful recipient. Every step of the process—from the rules of the wager, to the determination of the winner, to the transfer of money—is written into the distributed ledger by the miners for all to see. So long as the code is written correctly, there is no need for a middleman and no room for error.

A Better Way of Doing Business

Gambling is just one example of how powerful this technology can be. Another example is a musician foregoing the centralized, opaque, and expensive process of selling their music through a record label, choosing instead to do it on the blockchain. A smart contract could be created to take in payments in the form of cryptocoins from a buyer, and immediately send that buyer a token that contains a download key for a song. That same contract could further be programmed to take the money that comes in and immediately send it to the blockchain addresses of the people that helped create the song, according to a previously agreed-upon formula (i.e., the songwriter gets 20%, the singer 40%, the producer 10%, etc.).

The concept of a system of rules determining financial outcomes is at the core of many industries, from insurance to financial derivatives to international shipping. All of these industries currently require middlemen that charge significant premiums and add layers of risk and complexity. Smart contracts riding on a blockchain have the potential to make each of those industries cheaper, more efficient, and fairer than they've ever been.

A blockchain like Ethereum gives anyone the ability to create smart contracts and upload them to the network. A smart contract can even be programmed to reference a dapp that already exists on the blockchain, or to make transactions using a token. Smart contracts, in other words, can theoretically do a lot more than ordinary contracts. Some people believe that the ability to combine all of their features on the blockchain could create virtual entities that can someday replace certain corporations.

CONSIDER THIS

o The term "smart contract" was first coined in 1996 by computer scientist and legal scholar Nick Szabo, who is also the creator of Bit Gold, one of the first attempts at inventing digital money. Although Bit Gold was never implemented, many of its ideas were adopted by Satoshi Nakamoto to create Bitcoin.

o In blockchain parlance, a smart contract could be any kind of program that's executed on the ledger, even if it's not an electronic version of a traditional contract. There is also little technical distinction in practice between a smart contract and a dapp since, to the blockchain, both consist of a series of programming instructions.

o Smart contracts that facilitate gambling already exist on Ethereum, with different ones giving users the options to play a dice game, roulette, or blackjack. Unlike at a traditional casino, where you have to take the casino's word that the games are fair, users of such services can simply inspect their underlying code.

o In 2016, British pop star Imogen Heap released the song "Tiny Human" on Ethereum, using a smart contract that takes in payments in the form of ether and distributes the proceeds to various rights holders.

8

Decentralized Autonomous Organizations (DAOs)

A corporation is a legal entity that allows a group of people working together on a specific task to be treated as one. Creating a corporation involves setting up an ownership structure and management hierarchy and incorporating within a government jurisdiction that will then hold the company accountable to others. Corporations exist according to the code of law. Since blockchains replace the code of law with the law of code, they too can be used to create structured organizations devoted to specific tasks.

The simplest definition of a **decentralized autonomous organization**, or **DAO**, is a *programmed entity that exists in the jurisdiction of a blockchain, issues tokens to stakeholders, and fulfills functions governed by smart contracts.*

Whereas a regular corporation has shareholders, a DAO has token holders. Instead of being organized according to bylaws enforceable in court, DAOs have their structure executed in real time by smart contracts. They are *decentralized* because software does the work of officers, and *autonomous* because that software is executed by the blockchain.

Corporate Bylaws Replaced
by Computer Commands

DAOs replace the uncertainty of human discretion with the precise reliability of machines. This makes them a poor fit for corporate activities that require a lot of human decision-making, but a great disintermediary for the ones that don't. Some blockchain enthusiasts believe that eventually DAOs will replace some of the world's largest companies, depending on their purpose.

Take the example of a passive investment fund that pools money from individuals and makes investments according to a fixed formula, like an ETF that tracks a stock index. In traditional finance, such an investment company requires a group of managers and reams of legal paperwork to function, even though its mission is fairly straightforward and there are no hard decisions to be made.

The same fund could be executed more efficiently as a DAO on a blockchain. Shares issued by way of complicated legal papers are replaced by tokens issued by one smart contract, and managers tasked with following the preset investment formulas are replaced by other smart contracts that always do what they are supposed to. Banks and custodians are replaced by the built-in electronic money framework of the blockchain.

Using a DAO for this setup has the added benefit of full transparency. In a traditional investment scheme, confidence is found in the reputation of the managers and the certification provided by its outside auditors. If a manager makes a mistake or deliberately misappropriates funds, those affected might not find out until it's too late.

Since DAOs only do as they are programmed to, and can feature the full transparency of the blockchain, all their activities can be monitored by their token holders in real time, and any problem is apparent immediately.

A New Kind of Audit

DAOs shift the burden of outside verification from after the fact, as is the case with independent audits of the books of a traditional company, to before the fact, as is the case for independent audits of the code of any smart contract. Since everything on a blockchain happens in real time, making sure the code is designed and written well in the first place is crucial, as was proven by the first-ever decentralized autonomous organization on Ethereum.

Known as *The DAO*, it was designed to be an automated venture capital fund, and at the time the most ambitious project launched on the Ethereum blockchain. Participation was open to the public and anyone who sent The DAO's smart contracts ether via the blockchain was automatically sent back a token that represented their equity in the fund and the ability to vote on future projects. The tokens were to be freely traded on the secondary market, like stocks on the NASDAQ.

The DAO raised over $150 million in a matter of weeks, smashing all previously held records for crowdfunding projects. The staggering amount of money raised shined a spotlight on the Ethereum project, which was then relatively unknown, driving the price of ether up by 50% against the dollar, making the dollar value of the ether held by The DAO that much more valuable.

Investors celebrated the fact that for the first time ever, anyone investing in a venture capital fund could watch live as their money arrived at its destination, and that eventually they'd be able to watch the money leave and go to chosen projects they voted on, all without the need for the usual middlemen. The DAO's tokens started gaining in value against other currencies as soon as they started trading on cryptocoin exchanges, leading their owners to declare on Internet forums and social media that we were witnessing the dawn of a new era. Then it got hacked.

Within The DAO's smart contracts, someone found a flaw in the code that handled its ether and stole over a third of the money, transferring it to their own blockchain address. Thanks to the transparency of the Ethereum blockchain, where all transactions are recorded in real time for anyone to see, investors watched in horror as their money was taken. The value of The DAO's tokens crashed and ether lost a third of its value against the dollar.

The Downside of Decentralized

When a normal corporation gets robbed, its managers spring to action and call the authorities for help. But The DAO had no managers, and technically did not even exist in any particular country or legal jurisdiction. In a move reminiscent of the old Wild West, where self-appointed lawmen took on the role of protecting the innocent, a group of Ethereum developers used the same programming flaw to steal what remained of The DAOs ether before the thieves could take even more, putting it away for safekeeping until the community figured out what to do next.

The Dao disaster now serves as an important reminder that the power of blockchains and autonomous organizations can cut both ways. Despite the downsides of central authorities, one upside is that they can be called in to make important changes during an emergency.

The fatal flaw that doomed The DAO will not be the last software bug to cause a major disruption. Bugs are discovered in published software all the time, sometimes with potentially catastrophic results if left unaddressed. With traditional software, like Microsoft Windows, a central authority has the ability to issue a fix to every copy in use relatively quickly. Blockchains and smart contracts are not so easily updated.

But that's not to say that they can never be changed. There is a slow and decentralized way of updating everything on a blockchain, from the rules that govern it to the transactions it records, and it's called a fork.

o———————————————————————o

CONSIDER THIS

o When The DAO was first launched, many security
  experts warned that its smart contracts were not

designed well and were vulnerable to attack. Investors ignored them.

o The bug that was exploited by the hacker was, appropriately enough, found on line 666 of the smart contract code of The DAO. It was later determined that if a capital T in a command on that line had been lowercase, the theft would not have been possible.

o At the time of the hacking, The DAO held close to 14% of all the ether in existence.

o The $150 million valuation of The DAO's crowdfunding is based on taking the amount of ether it held and multiplying it by the then price of ether in dollars. Given the appreciation of the cryptocoin since then, had The DAO not been hacked, its ether today would be worth over $10 billion, making it one of the bigger venture capital funds out there.

9

Forks

The Ethereum community was plunged into an existential crisis after The DAO disaster of 2016, as different parties argued what, if anything, should be done about the theft. The vulnerability that the thief exploited gave him or her the ability to transfer millions of dollar's worth of ether into a separate account, but due to a lucky technical quirk, it prevented them from accessing the money for 30 days. The countdown was on to find a solution.

Blockchain purists argued that the matter should be left alone, because The DAO's problems were not Ethereum's. They believed that bad smart contracts and faulty DAOs were an unavoidable risk when living by the law of code, and that the platform itself had behaved as intended, even for the hackers. Some even argued that the programmers who wrote the faulty smart contracts were more to blame than the actual thieves.

Ethereum's core development team on the other hand, led by its founder, believed that a heist that put so many coins into the hands of a malevolent actor was a dangerous state of affairs for such a young blockchain. Shortly before the one-month window closed, they proposed repossessing the stolen funds by altering a part of the ledger.

Changing the Ledger

One way of thinking of a blockchain is as an official time-line of events that participants continuously come to agree on. Miners are the historians who process the latest develop-ments, be they transactions or programming instructions, and nodes are the archivists, keeping and constantly updating a record of everything that's ever happened. Every new block that's created contains both the latest entrants into the his-tory books and the rules by which they were admitted.

The simplest definition of a blockchain **fork** is *a change at a specific block that creates an alternate version of history.*

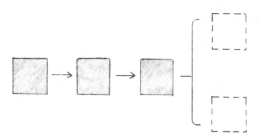

Figure 07.
A Potential Change in the Timeline

Most forks are accidental and temporary. Since the pro-cess of writing the ledger is decentralized, different min-ers are always competing to be the first to solve the latest math puzzle so they can create the next block and collect its reward. Sometimes, two miners complete the puzzle at almost the same time, and present the community with two slightly different lists of transactions, creating a fork. The consensus mechanism then kicks in and picks the block that is the most representative version of history, while the other one is deemed **orphaned** and ignored by the rest of the network.

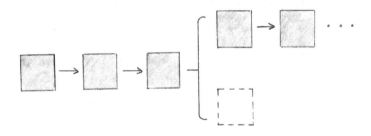

Figure 08. An Orphaned Block

A Decentralized Upgrade

Forks can also be intentional and used to upgrade the rules by which a blockchain operates. In a decentralized network, change can only occur democratically. If a majority of nodes and miners agree to operate by a new set of rules as of a specific block, then the chain automatically forks from that point on, creating a new timeline.

Upgrade forks are often preplanned, and some of the newer blockchains, like Ethereum, began with a road map that called for specific upgrade forks when certain milestones

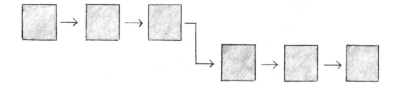

Figure 09.
Upgrading the Rules of the Blockchain

were hit. The changes they implement usually have to do
with how the blockchain functions and the rules of the consensus mechanism. Such forks come in two varieties: soft
and hard. The difference between them is subtle, so much
so that they can even confuse people with a programming
background.

A **soft fork** is *a change to the consensus rules of a blockchain where the set of rules that govern its transactions are
shaved to be more limiting going forward.*

A simple example would be a blockchain that used to accept
transactions in fractions being forked to now accept only whole
numbers. Since mathematically speaking 5 is the same as 5.00
to a computer, any node going by the old rules will still accept
all transactions written using the new method. For this reason,
soft forks are always backward compatible, like buying a new
Playstation console that can still play games from older Playsta-
tions. Soft forks only need to be adopted by a simple majority
of the nodes of a blockchain to become official.

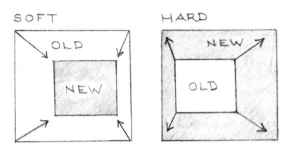

Figure 10. Two Kinds of Forks

A **hard fork** is *a change to the consensus rules of a block-chain where the rules that govern its transactions are grown to be more accepting going forward.*

Changing a blockchain that used to only accept whole numbers to now accept fractions is a much more drastic step, because any node that has not upgraded to the new rules is going to reject new transactions with decimals as invalid. That means hard forks are not backward compatible, akin to buying an Xbox that won't accept any of your Playstation games. Since hard forks are a much more drastic upgrade, they need virtually unanimous adoption by all the participants of the chain to go into effect.

An Emergency Upgrade

To undo the DAO heist, Ethereum's core developers called for adding new programming instructions to the ledger that would take the stolen ether and transfer it to a new smart contract that would issue refunds to those who invested in The DAO. Since adding new commands that didn't exist before is an expansion of the old rules, what Vitalik Buterin and his team were asking the community to vote on was an emergency hard fork.

Voting in proof-of-work blockchains like Ethereum and Bitcoin is not done per person or organization, but rather per **hash power**, a technical term that means *the amount of computing power available to solve the math puzzle and process new transactions at any given point in time.*

Proof of work exists to maintain the integrity of a blockchain. By forcing anyone who wants to become a writer of new blocks to have to expend costly computing power first, the mechanism weeds out malevolent actors. When it comes to voting on a potential fork, this mechanism also helps prevent any single participant from stuffing the ballot. How much of a vote any miner gets during a fork is simply a product of how much hash power they possess and dedicate to the new rules.

In July of 2016, at block number 1,920,000, most of the Ethereum blockchain's hashing power forked to rescue The DAO. The transition was relatively painless, and the fork's supporters (many of which were investors in The DAO) flooded chat rooms and social media with congratulatory posts to each other and praise for the core development team.

Unfortunately for them, when it comes to hard forks, *most* isn't good enough. A small minority of Ethereum's hash power, controlled by miners who believed blockchains should be immutable and not altered to bail out individual users, continued operating by the old set of rules. In doing so, and refusing to accept an altered version of history, they helped create two parallel blockchains.

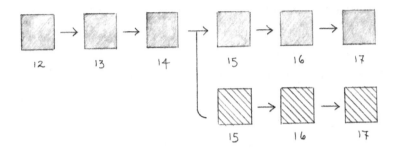

Figure 11. A Chain Split

Chain Splits Create
Two Different Blockchains

In the altered, or forked chain, the one that we still call Ethereum today, the DAO disaster was unwound, and the stolen coins were taken out of the thieves' account and put in a smart contract that allowed the original investors to claim a refund. But in the other chain, the one we now call Ethereum Classic, nothing changed, and the thieves kept the loot.

Today, both Ethereum and Ethereum Classic exist as thriving, though independent, blockchains. If you look at the transactions and smart contracts being processed by either network right now, they will look very different, as will some of the rules by which they are processed. But if you start walking back through their respective ledgers, you'll see that at some point they become identical, because prior to the fork, they have a shared history.

Other than the changes that were the subject of a hard fork in the first place, chain splits create two identical blockchains. Anyone who owned ether on the Ethereum blockchain at the moment of the split ended up owning the same exact amount of ether classic on the other blockchain as well, because the public addresses and private keys all stayed the same.

Since then however, the two chains have evolved differently. By retaining the core development team and the majority of the mining hash power, Ethereum has become one of the most valuable blockchains after Bitcoin, and is an important development platform for the most mainstream dapps being created today.

Ethereum Classic is a much smaller platform, mostly used by experimental developers to build niche dapps. Its biggest selling point is its strict adherence to immutability, or the idea that neither the current transactions in the ledger nor its rules of operation will ever be altered to benefit specific users.

The unintended split of Ethereum into two different blockchains is a reminder that much is unpredictable in this new and exciting domain, especially when developers take an existing platform and try to improve upon it, as is the case in the ongoing Bitcoin scaling debate.

CONSIDER THIS

o The Ethereum hard fork that failed to reach full consensus and resulted in the split still had 89% participation. The fact that just 11% of the hash rate not going along was enough to split the chain is a good reminder of how precarious this style of upgrade can be.

o The DAO thief stole approximately 3.5 million ether. Had Ethereum never been forked to recover those funds, today the thief would be a billionaire. Luckily for him, he still got to keep the coins in the Ethereum Classic blockchain where the fork was never implemented, as that bounty is still worth over $100 million.

o Who the thief actually was has never been discovered. In an ironic twist, he or she donated some of the stolen coins to a new development team that took over Ethereum Classic after the fork.

o Given the trauma of the chain-split, Vitalik Buterin has since said that if he had to do it all over again, he'd let things be and not try the emergency hard fork.

10

Scaling

All blockchains have a scaling problem. Since they are designed to be trust-building platforms, they prioritize security ahead of everything else, including efficiency. Compared to other digital networks, blockchains are very slow.

The Bitcoin blockchain currently averages four transactions per second. If the cryptocoin is to ever be considered a viable alternative to paper money for day-to-day purchases, its blockchain is going to have to be scaled to handle a lot more. This is no easy task, because much of what makes a blockchain like Bitcoin's viable is also what makes it slow.

The first issue is the decentralized nature of most blockchains. This means that thousands of nodes around the world, some of which don't have the fastest Internet access, need a chance to download the latest blocks before new ones are mined.

Then there is Bitcoin's proof-of-work mechanism and the computational work that miners have to do to write every new block. Most of the time it takes to mine a block is spent trying to solve the puzzle, as opposed to writing the transactions into the ledger. The delay is intentional.

Satoshi Nakamoto designed Bitcoin to average writing one block every 10 minutes. The purpose is to make it harder for malicious actors to write bad transactions before others might notice. Although actual block times can vary from a few minutes to an hour, the mining algorithm is programmed to regularly adjust to maintain that 10-minute average.

Regulating the Speed of a Blockchain

The rate at which Bitcoin blocks are created is influenced by several factors. One is the number of pending transactions. If nobody sends or receives any Bitcoins for a while, there's no reason to write a new block. Then there is the availability of miners and how much computing power they possess. If there is only one miner with limited hash power, it will take a long time to solve the math puzzle.

It helps to think of the mining process as the ticket line at a train station. If there are a lot of passengers wanting to buy tickets at the same time, a queue will form. How fast that queue moves is dependent on how many ticket windows are open, along with how long it takes for each window to issue new tickets. In Blockchain parlance, that last variable is called the difficulty.

The simplest definition of a blockchain's **difficulty** is *the amount of computational work it takes to solve the math puzzle before a new block can be mined.* The higher the difficulty, the more work that miners have to do to solve the puzzle, so the longer it takes to create each new block.

When designing Bitcoin, Nakamoto understood that the rate of transactions (people who want to buy a ticket) and the mining hash power (number of available windows) would fluctuate over time. To try to regulate the process, and to maintain a consistent rate of block creation, he introduced an adjustable difficulty (the time it takes to issue each train ticket). Every few weeks, the Bitcoin mining algorithm looks at how busy the network has been and how much mining power has been available, then adjusts the difficulty to try to maintain the 10-minute block time.

None of this would impact the transaction throughput of the blockchain if every new block could handle an infinite number of transactions, but there is a cap.

Hitting Capacity

Every Bitcoin block has a limit of how much information it can contain before miners have to move on to the next one. For technical reasons, that limit is in the amount of computer memory each block takes up, and it is currently set at approximately one megabyte. Nakamoto originally designed Bitcoin's blockchain with a much bigger block size, but that made it vulnerable to spam attacks, so in 2010 he led the community in a fork that brought the limit down drastically. Bitcoin was not as popular back then, so the smaller block size was still enough to contain every pending transaction.

But over the years, as adoption grew, so did the number of transactions per block, until the network started hitting the one-megabyte limit regularly, forcing some transactions to have to wait for subsequent blocks to be confirmed. This queue can form regardless of the mining difficulty or the availability of hash power, akin to a train station having a preset limit on how many tickets it's willing to sell because there aren't enough trains.

Soaring Costs

Whenever Bitcoin hits the block size limit, transaction costs start to climb, because unlike our existing banking system, the Bitcoin blockchain doesn't have fixed fees. Instead, each user can decide how much they want to pay the miners to have their transaction processed, and each miner can in turn pick which transactions it wants to process. Bitcoin miners are for-profit entities that, along with the new coins generated by the mining algorithm with each passing block, also get to collect the transaction fees in that block. To maximize their profits, they always process the transactions that pay the highest fees first.

This is not an issue when the network isn't at capacity, because each new block can contain every pending transaction. But whenever the network gets busy, some transactions have to wait until the next block to be processed, forcing those that want immediate processing to pay higher fees to jump to the head of the line. The experience is a lot like the congestion pricing model used by ride sharing services like Uber.

Back before the blockchain started hitting the size limit, the average transaction cost for sending bitcoins was in the pennies. That number started to climb in 2016, and by the spring of 2017 was averaging $2, sometimes spiking all the way to $5. Users who wanted to still pay low fees had to wait hours, if not days, to have their transactions processed by the miners.

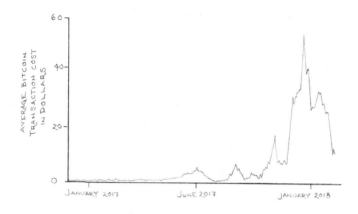

Figure 12. Surging Transaction Costs

Since low transaction costs are meant to be a key selling point for cryptocoin adoption, Bitcoin's scaling issue boiled over into a crisis, with different parties proposing different solutions and getting into heated debates. Just as with the Ethereum hard fork debate, blockchain purists argued that nothing should be done, and if Bitcoin was expensive to use during periods of peak activity, so be it. Others were worried high fees would deter the technology from ever going mainstream, and proposed various scaling solutions, most of which fell into two camps: one advocating bigger blocks and the other for a different infrastructure.

The Community Begins to Fragment

Increasing the size of every block is the simplest solution. Bigger blocks can store more transactions, the functional equivalent of a train station switching to bigger trains that can carry more people. The downside of doing so is that it would make the ledger bigger, and thus harder to store, driving away smaller nodes, and making the overall network less decentralized. On the plus side, the user experience would remain the same. There would still be the occasional backlog, but thanks to the bigger capacity of each block, it would clear quickly.

The other proposal was to build additional infrastructure with the goal of moving smaller transactions off the blockchain and onto a peripheral network. Such a network would handle batches of small transactions on its own, then report back to the blockchain for occasional verification. Transactions sent on the peripheral network would be fast and cheap, but not as trustworthy as ones on the main chain. Users would then be offered a choice for each transaction.

Improving a technology that lacks a decision-making central authority is a messy process. Bitcoin's Core Development team, a group of volunteers that has led the way in most of its past upgrades, is generally opposed to block size increases, arguing that Bitcoin should be reserved for large transactions where the need for trust supersedes speed or cost. Large miners on the other hand, who worry that transactions moved off-chain to a peripheral network would hurt their revenues, and small-time users who can't afford higher fees, have often called for larger block sizes.

In May of 2017, a large consortium of cryptocoin businesses from around the world, including exchanges, vendors, and service providers, proposed a compromise solution, known colloquially as *the New York Agreement,* to deploy both solutions.

First, a soft fork would be initiated to introduce a technical upgrade called Segregated Witness (SegWit for short), opening the door for peripheral networks. Several months later, the block size would be doubled to two megabytes, via a hard fork.

As is the case for most compromises, not everyone was pleased.

A Twin Is Born   *Bitcoin Cash*

The leaders of a major mining pool responsible for one-third of all Bitcoin mining argued that even a two-megabyte block size was not enough, and that the same capacity problems were bound to show up again, unless something drastic was done. So in the summer of 2017, they took matters into their own hands and unilaterally initiated a hard fork to increase the block size not just to two megabytes, but to eight, quadrupling the network's block capacity.

This faction, which also included a handful of defectors from Bitcoin's original development team, knew all along that the majority of the blockchain's hash power would never support such a radical fork. Their goal was to intentionally force a chain split and, given the amount of hash power they possessed, they succeeded in doing so, creating a new cryptocurrency which they called Bitcoin Cash. The original Bitcoin blockchain continued as it had before, and its remaining community successfully soft forked to include the SegWit upgrade.

Today, Bitcoin Cash is one of the most valuable cryptocurrencies in the world. Aside from having a larger block size, and no SegWit, Cash is identical to Bitcoin in almost every way.

The two coins share an identical history before the fork, and just as with the 2016 split in Ethereum, anyone that owned bitcoins going into the fork ended up owning equivalent amounts of Cash.

Crypto Clone Wars

The split of Bitcoin Cash from Bitcoin has turned out to be a seminal event in the life of the cryptocurrency. Debates between the two factions still rage on, and often sound more political than technical. On the one hand, supporters of Bitcoin Cash, often referred to as *big blockers*, have been on a crusade to convince the community that since their coin still offers insignificant transaction costs, it is the true heir to Nakamoto's original vision of digital money that can be used for day-to-day transactions.

The Bitcoin Core Development team, on the other hand, has grown even more entrenched in their belief that high transaction costs on the Bitcoin blockchain are not a problem, so much so that they refused to back the second step of the New York Agreement, which called for a hard fork of the original chain to a two-megabyte block size. Their opposition was so strong that in the fall of 2017 the authors of the compromise agreement decided to postpone that fork indefinitely, for fear of yet another chain split.

Such decisions have sealed the fate of the original Bitcoin chain, at least for now, as one of higher fees. Peripheral networks that handle transactions off-chain are only in an early stage of development. Nobody can be certain that they will work, and even if they do, they are months, if not years, away from implementation. In the meantime, as the original Bitcoin's popularity has continued to grow, so have its transaction costs, at times averaging over $20 per transaction, or more than a wire from a bank.

All currencies fulfill multiple functions, but some are tailored for one purpose more than others. The original Bitcoin's growing transaction costs have made it more of a *store of value* and less a *medium of exchange*, opening the door for other cryptocurrencies, including Bitcoin Cash, to compete for the job of digital money that can be used for microtransactions. That competition continues to play out in the ever-changing landscape of altcoins.

CONSIDER THIS

○ Nakamoto originally designed Bitcoin with a 36-megabyte block size, then reduced it to just one megabyte, as the higher number made the network vulnerable to certain kinds of attack. One of his last suggestions before disappearing was to eventually set the blockchain so the block size would automatically increase over time.

○ Since Bitcoin and Bitcoin Cash are so similar, anyone set up to mine one can easily mine the other, and many miners work on both, switching their hash power back and forth, depending on which coin is more profitable.

o During periods of peak activity, some Bitcoin users who want their transaction to be mined immediately end up paying more in fees than the money they are moving.

o The success of the Bitcoin Cash fork in creating a viable cryptocurrency has led many copycats to attempt the same thing, but with their own unique quirks. Examples include Bitcoin Gold, Bitcoin Diamond, and Segwit2x.

o Bitcoin is not the only blockchain with capacity problems. During periods of peak activity, Ethereum can get bogged down as well, and scaling is generally a much bigger problem for blockchains that can also handle programming instructions.

11

Alt Coins

Bitcoin is many things. It's a currency, a new way of storing and transferring value, and a collection of technologies. One reason people have a hard time understanding it is because it exists thanks to a variety of concepts, taken from the only tangentially related fields of programming, economics, and game theory. Most of those concepts are rather abstract, so specific answers to significant questions are hard to come by. There are no fixed rules of which consensus mechanism works best, how many new coins should be created each year, or what is the optimum block size of a blockchain.

Since Satoshi Nakamoto's launch of the original implementation, other developers have shown up with their own ideas of how to best structure a blockchain or manage a purely digital form of money. Some of these developers have tried to simply improve on the original, while others have applied the concept of a blockchain to areas other than money. There are now dozens of cryptocurrencies out there, and if you include tokens riding the Ethereum blockchain, the number runs into the thousands.

Given the sheer size, age, and popularity of Bitcoin, all other coins are collectively called **alt coins**. The nomenclature is appropriate enough, as many of the biggest altcoins started out by copying Bitcoin's core software or directly forking off its blockchain. There is no specific method for classifying altcoin projects, bust most of them can be placed in several broad categories.

Digital Money

Most of the major altcoins attempt to take what Bitcoin does—using a distributed ledger to track transactions processed by miners who follow a consensus mechanism—and improve upon it. Cryptocurrencies such as Bitcoin Cash, Litecoin, Dash, and Monero each take the original idea and significantly alter at least one attribute.

Litecoin for example advertises itself as "the silver to Bitcoin's gold." Its faster block times and looser inflation schedule make it more of a means of exchange than a store of value. Dash implements a unique governance model where so-called *masternodes*—nodes that must put money in escrow with the blockchain—get a greater say in how the blockchain is run, and in return collect a portion of the mining reward. Monero offers far more anonymity.

The values of these cryptocurrencies have fluctuated wildly in recent years as the market has tried to sort out which set of features is most useful. Altcoin price moves often result from developments with Bitcoin that might make one of its core attributes stand out as a positive or negative. Bitcoin Cash and Litecoin, for example, have at times climbed in value as Bitcoin's transaction costs have spiked, while Monero has gained prominence following instances of Bitcoin's transparency leading to criminal prosecutions.

Smart Contract Platforms

The second most popular kind of altcoin are ones like Ethereum, whose blockchains can handle programming instructions alongside cryptocoin transactions. Such blockchains also grapple with questions to which there is no single right answer, like what programming language participants should use to write a smart contract, or what kind of consensus mechanism can execute such contracts most efficiently. Given the success of Ethereum in recent years, the other major smart contract platforms often try to define themselves by how they differ.

EOS, for example, has functionality that in an emergency like The DAO hacking would allow the creators of a smart contract to modify it. Cardano separates the processing of coin transactions from the processing of programming instructions into two different blockchain layers, making it easier to upgrade one functionality without touching the other. NEO has features that allow its smart contracts to be better connected to physical objects in the real world.

Scaling is a major challenge for smart contract platforms, even more so than for pure cryptocurrencies. Moving money from one blockchain address to another requires just one transaction, while even a simple smart contract might require many. To speed up their blockchains, all of these examples do away with the proof-of-work mechanism altogether, opting for a more efficient consensus mechanism known as **proof of stake**.

That mechanism does away with the need for miners to do hard core computation to prove their good intentions, and instead simply asks them to put a bunch of coins in escrow *PoS* with the blockchain, or *at stake*. If a miner writes the next block honestly, it gets a reward. But if it tries anything malicious, it loses the escrow. Eliminating the need to do hard core computation or solving the math puzzle increases the speed and efficiency of a blockchain, making it a better mechanism for one meant to be a world computer. Even Ethereum is expected to eventually migrate from proof-of-work mining to a proof-of-stake model.

Utility Tokens

The vast majority of cryptocurrencies out there today are utility tokens, designed to facilitate a specific operation. Some of these tokens have their own blockchain, while others ride on smart contract platforms that have a built-in token functionality.

The most valuable utility tokens are built to do something similar to what Bitcoin does, and help transfer value via a blockchain. But instead of they themselves being the stores of value, they help transport other digital assets. Ripple, for example, is the utility token for the Ripple Network, a proposed upgrade to our aging banking infrastructure. Its creators believe that the best application of blockchain technology is not to replace the existing banking system, but to upgrade it, by giving banks a new way of sending assets—be they dollars, stocks, or even Bitcoins—back and forth between each other. Ripple tokens are then used to pay a sort of toll on this blockchain-based asset highway.

There are many other utility tokens that exist to serve a similar function. OmisGO aims to use a blockchain to replace remittance services like Western Union, and NEM allows financial companies to develop their own in-house ledger, then connect it via a blockchain to that of another company.

Then there are the utility tokens that hope to usher in the next generation of the sharing economy. In the same spirit of Uber giving you access to someone else's car and Airbnb giving you access to someone else's home, Siacoins let you rent space on someone else's hard drive, while Golem lets you rent out your computer's spare processing power.

Since blockchain technology was originally invented to create trust where it wouldn't otherwise exist, it's the perfect solution for any project that requires strangers to interact with each other. Brainstorm any business that falls into that category, from an online casino to a smart-grid for electricity, and odds are there is already a utility token trying to facilitate the concept. Whether such tokens should in and of themselves have much value, or any at all, is a hotly debated subject.

Who Will Prevail

Altcoins are a fascinating window into the future, and it's easy to get excited about the possibility of each unique project. For a more detailed analysis and explanation of some of the biggest altcoins, you can visit the appendix at the end of this book. But for now, it's important to remember that technological revolutions are inherently hard to predict. If history is any guide, most of the projects just listed will eventually fail, and some of the future's most successful blockchain projects have yet to be invented.

The wisest thing for any outside participant to do at this juncture is to keep learning about the space and its various implementations, and there is no better way to learn than by going through the practical experience.

CONSIDER THIS

○ Altcoins are often ranked by their market cap, a method of measuring a cryptocurrency's overall value by multiplying the number of coins currently in circulation by the dollar value of each coin.

○ A popular website for tracking the market cap of each altcoin, www.coinmarketcap.com, currently lists over 1,300 different coins and tokens.

○ One indication of how much busier smart contract platforms can be as compared to simple cryptocoin ones is that, as of January of 2018, the Ethereum blockchain processes more transactions per day than all other blockchains, including Bitcoin, combined.

o The other appeal of proof of stake mining over proof of work is the environmental impact, as the electrical usage of proof of work across multiple blockchains is significant and growing.

12

The User Experience

I nteracting with a blockchain starts and ends with an address, as the technology is just a database that keeps track of hundreds of thousands of addresses and their cryptocoin balances. On Ethereum and other smart contract platforms, an address might also contain tokens or programming instructions. Addresses on most blockchains are a long string of letters and numbers, and the software that controls them can generate an infinite number of new ones.

Each address has its own **private key**, a sort of password that looks like an even longer string of letters and numbers, and grants access to the contents of that particular address. Every time a blockchain generates a new address, it also generates its private key. The easiest way for you to get a new address is by installing a cryptocoin wallet.

The simplest definition of a cryptocoin **wallet** is *software that stores your address and private key and interacts with the blockchain on your behalf.*

Holding and Sending Coins

Wallets can be installed on your computer or smartphone, or run via a third-party website. Most blockchains have an

0x06012cf97BEaD5deAe237070F9587f8E7A266d

1A1zP1eP5QGefi2DMPTfTL5SLmv7DivfNa

Figure 13. Sample Addresses

official wallet created by their development team, but since the software that controls the blockchain is open-source, there are usually third-party options as well. Once you install a wallet and have it generate a new address and private key, you are free to share the address with anyone that wants to send you money. Your private key on the other hand should always be kept a secret, because once it's compromised, there is no way to change it.

New coins can be acquired by having someone send you some, or by purchasing them through a cryptocoin exchange.

The simplest definition of a **cryptocoin exchange** is *a business that facilitates buyers and sellers coming together to trade cryptocoins against each other or against paper forms of money.* Such exchanges are similar to existing exchanges for financial products like stocks, with the added functionality of being able to interact with the blockchains of the cryptocurrencies they trade.

Cryptocoin exchanges come in two varieties. **Centralized exchanges** allow users to keep their coins stored at the exchange, while **decentralized exchanges** only facilitate a buyer and seller interacting via the blockchain. The former act a lot like your existing online stock broker, while the latter are more akin to using Craigslist to find someone you can trade with directly.

Once you've acquired your coins on an exchange or from another user, you can transfer them to your own blockchain address. Any funds sent to that address will eventually appear in your wallet, but the coins won't actually reside there, as they only exist as entries in the ledger. A wallet that "holds a balance" is simply passing on information it downloaded from one of the nodes in the blockchain. Most wallets have the capacity to track multiple addresses for the same cryptocoin, and some can even track different coins on different blockchains.

Sending coins out of your address is done by telling your wallet the recipient's address and how much money you want to send. Some wallets let you choose how much in fees you'd like to pay the miners, while others go with a preset amount. For added security, most wallets also ask you for a pin code

Figure 14.

A Typical Cryptocoin Wallet

FRAUD

or password that you would have set up locally on your device when you first installed the software.

Once you confirm the details and click send, your wallet will transmit your transaction to the blockchain, using your private key as proof that you are the rightful owner. For you, this is the end of the process. But for the blockchain and the recipient of your transaction, it's only the beginning.

From Pending to Accepted

Depending on the blockchain you are using, its current level of activity, and the fees you paid, your transaction may take anywhere from a few seconds to an hour to be processed by a miner and entered into the ledger for the first time. At this point, it is said to have one confirmation.

Confirmations on a blockchain are *the number of blocks mined so far that have validated your transaction.*

Before processing your transaction, the miner that's writing it into the ledger for the first time traces the history of the coins you are sending to confirm that you are their rightful owner. This verification is done each time anyone sends a coin, and the cumulative effect is that every transaction verifies all the ones that came before it, so every new block confirms all preceding blocks. Whenever a new block is added to the chain, all existing transactions in the ledger gain an additional confirmation.

Most blockchain participants require seeing more than one block confirmation before they consider a transaction valid, out of fear of forks and malicious attacks. Because anyone can sign up to be a miner, it's theoretically possible for a hacker to

FRAUD

submit a bogus transaction and mine it themselves, automatically getting one confirmation.

The proof-of-work mechanism is designed to root out such behavior, but doing so takes time, or more specifically, blocks. One component of the math puzzle that every miner (including our thief) has to complete to write the next block is a guessing game, similar to roulette. This feature is designed to make sure the same miner rarely gets to write multiple blocks in a row. The thief might win this game for one block but is unlikely to keep winning for future blocks. As soon as a different miner wins the game, they will discover the bad transaction and alert the rest of the network.

With every new block that is mined, the odds of a fraudulent transaction surviving falls exponentially. In the Bitcoin blockchain, that likelihood goes to zero after six blocks, so most recipients, especially those receiving large transactions, don't consider a transaction valid until it has six confirmations. They can always wait for even more, because this process never stops. So long as the Bitcoin blockchain continues to add new blocks, all existing transactions continue collecting confirmations.

This entire process is on display for anyone to see. Not only does your wallet and that of the recipient track and display the mining and confirmation process as it happens, but anyone that knows either of your addresses can enter it into a website dedicated to exploring the blockchain and get the same information. The only exception to this third-party transparency are blockchains designed for added privacy.

Most of today's cryptocoin wallets are designed to resemble interfaces you are already used to from the current banking system. Once you understand how a blockchain works and what confirmations are, using a crypto wallet is no different than using your bank's mobile app, unless of course you make a mistake.

CONSIDER THIS

o Decentralized exchanges often allow users to transact with each other anonymously, only ever having to disclose their blockchain address. This means you could exchange one cryptocurrency for another without ever having to disclose your identity.

o Wallets that don't allow you to set a custom transaction fee became problematic for users when Bitcoin's capacity issues caused transaction prices to skyrocket. Since such wallets tended to be older, the default fee they included in each transaction was often too low by contemporary standards, causing their coins to get stuck in the queue for days on end.

o Since every new block on a blockchain confirms all previous blocks, and Bitcoin is the oldest blockchain, the earliest Bitcoin transactions have by now been confirmed close to half a million times.

o Since different blockchains have different block times, the number of confirmations needed to consider a transaction valid varies from one coin to another. Ethereum transactions often need at least 12 and sometimes up to 20 block confirmations to be accepted as valid.

13

Mistakes

For money to have value, each discrete unit must be irreplicable. You have confidence in the dollars in your possession because nobody can duplicate those bills. But as a necessary trade-off, you can't call the U.S. mint for a replacement if you lose your wallet.

The great breakthrough of blockchain technology is that it gives cryptocoins the same attribute, making them the first irreplicable digital asset. But as many crypto early adopters have learned the hard way, for something to be irreplicable, it must also be irreplaceable, including when it's lost or stolen.

The emergency hard fork that Ethereum's developers enacted to recover the stolen DAO funds was a rare exception in that regard, and one that came at such a cost that its development team eventually concluded was a mistake. Cryptocoin thefts usually play out as they did on the Ethereum Classic blockchain, where the thieves just kept the money.

Platforms like Ethereum are often targeted by thieves and hackers because the complexity of the smart contracts they host increases the odds of a security hole. They will be targeted even more once they gain widespread adoption. But that's not to say that they are the only targets, as there have been spectacular thefts all over the blockchain sector.

Bank Robbers

In 2014, a Japanese company named Mt. Gox, then the largest cryptocoin exchange in the world and accounting for 70% of all Bitcoin purchases, abruptly went bankrupt. Its clients soon learned that an unknown hacker who had penetrated the company's servers had been stealing their coins for months, eventually walking away with an astonishing 850,000 bitcoins, or almost 7% of all bitcoins in circulation at that time. The blockchain's built-in privacy features made it almost impossible to figure out who the thief was. The sheer size of the theft was so shocking that it sent the price of the cryptocoin crashing at other exchanges around the world, eventually losing 80% of its value.

Centralized cryptocoin exchanges where users buy, sell, and store their coins are obvious targets for hackers, and despite their dedicating massive resources to security, breaches still happen all the time. The collapse of Mt. Gox left a centralized exchange named Bitfinex as the world's busiest Bitcoin exchange. In 2016 they were also hacked, with the thieves walking away with almost 120,000 coins.

Such attacks are the primary reason why most security experts recommend not storing your coins in any place other than a private wallet where only you possess the private key. The better you secure that private key, the safer your coins. But as anyone who has ever created a password that was so complicated they couldn't remember it the next day can attest, there's a downside to being too secure.

A Very Expensive Oops

Look through the archives of message boards dedicated to cryptocoins and you'll come across countless posts by panicked people who can no longer access their own coins, even though technically speaking the money is still in their address.

The safest way to store your private key is on a so-called paper wallet, literally writing it down on a piece of paper that you store somewhere safe. Forget where you put that piece of paper, and your coins might as well be gone.

Another option is to use a software wallet that holds your private key and secures it with an additional password. This is a common feature on most wallets running on devices that are connected to the Internet, like laptops and smartphones, because it prevents an unauthorized user or a computer virus from stealing your key. Forget your wallet password, and your coins might as well be gone.

Digital storage of a private key has its own risks. Flash drives can go bad and hard drives can fail, taking keys for which there's no backup copy with them. In the early days of Bitcoin, when each coin was worth only a few cents, many developers bought thousands of them to play around with, then moved on to other projects, forgetting about their private keys. Years later, when the price of each coin was in the thousands, some had to go scouring through basements and attics, looking for the hard drive whose contents might buy them a house.

Just as people have accidentally come across old paintings worth millions of dollars at garage sales, the day will come when someone happens upon an old computer with a private key that will make them rich.

Blockchains like Bitcoin and Ethereum have a predictable inflation schedule, meaning an algorithm decides how many new coins are created each year. But the actual number of coins in circulation is always lower than the algorithm would indicate, because every year, thousands of coins are lost. The blockchain still knows where they are, because every coin is just an entry in the ledger, but practically speaking, coins that can no longer be accessed by a user are like treasure on a sunken ship at the bottom of the ocean, and might as well not exist.

On top of making storage mistakes, cryptocoin users are also vulnerable to errors made in the process of making transactions via the blockchain. For each transaction that you initiate, the blockchain only cares if the particular parameters you enter—like the recipient's address—are *valid*. Whether that information is in fact *correct* is a whole other matter.

Copying and pasting the wrong address in the Recipient box of a wallet is not unheard of, nor is meaning to send 5 coins with 0.05 in transaction fees but accidentally swapping the two numbers. One mistake benefits a lucky stranger while the other pays unnecessary fees to a miner. Neither is reversible, and in both cases the blockchain did its job. Those misdirected coins are as usable as a twenty-dollar bill found on the sidewalk.

The Downside of Decentralized

If an outside observer didn't know better, stories like the ones just mentioned would make them think that blockchain users are more prone to these kinds of mishaps than the general population. But crashed hard drives and forgotten passwords happen to people in all walks of life. It's only in the context of a completely decentralized platform designed to make transactions irreversible that such mistakes can become catastrophic.

You've probably forgotten other important passwords in the past, but because help has always been a *Forgot Password?* link away, the impact was negligible. But as cryptocoin users are fond of saying, mistakes on a blockchain, like diamonds, are forever.

Ultimately, the cost of such mistakes is a testament to the power of this new technology. If losing something or having it stolen hurts, then it must be valuable. That value has many benevolent applications, from payments to computing to digital rights management. But just as with dollars and gold and anything else that's ever been valuable, there is also a downside.

CONSIDER THIS

o Had the hard fork to reverse The DAO theft never been enacted, the value of the stolen ether would today be in the billions of dollars.

o Even though the Mt. Gox hacker made away with most of the exchange's coins, the parabolic appreciation in

the price of Bitcoin since then means that the minority of coins that weren't stolen, and are currently held
by the bankruptcy trustee, are now worth more than
the then value of the coins that were stolen.

o Users having missing letters or typos in their wallet
passwords is such a common problem that there is
a service which will try to guess your mistake, by
using an advanced algorithm run on powerful cloud
computers. The service only works if your actual
password is close to what you think it is, and charges
20% of the contents of the wallet should it succeed.

o There is one way to try to void a mistaken transaction, which is to use the blockchain's built-in anti
double-spend feature. So long as your transaction
hasn't been confirmed yet, you can send the same
coins to yourself while paying a higher fee. Miners
will process the more profitable self-transaction first,
then reject the mistake as a double spend.

14

Crypto Cons

The first time many people heard of a cryptocoin was in the spring of 2013, when the U.S. government took down the notorious Silk Road dark-web bazaar, which was a market for drugs and other illicit products. News reports of the event mentioned that in the process of arresting the site's founder, the FBI confiscated over 300,000 bitcoins.

Cryptocoins have gotten a lot of negative press in their relatively young history. Some of that negative attention is justified, like with the WannaCry cryptoworm, which infected hundreds of thousands of computers around the world and locked up their hard drives, demanding users pay a ransom in bitcoins. The virus was so pervasive that it shut down certain parts of the National Health Service in Britain.

Sensational stories of such events, often written by journalists who don't necessarily understand the underlying technology, have painted a negative image of this nascent space as something to be leery of. And while it's true that the decentralized nature of Bitcoin or the privacy features of Monero make them appealing to criminals, blaming the currency for allowing the crime is akin to saying there's something wrong with the dollar because of the Madoff Ponzi scheme.

Cat and Mouse

If you look at it in a historical context, cryptocoins are no different from other technological revolutions when criminals looking to gain an edge on law enforcement were early adopters, if not outright pioneers.

During Prohibition, bootleggers trying to outrun the cops became so good at making cars go fast that their recreational weekend races eventually turned into NASCAR. More recently, when primitive mobile communication in the form of beepers and pagers first hit the market, drug dealers were among the first businessmen to incorporate them for regular use. That association was so strong, it was often mentioned in the popular music of the time.

Today, fast cars and mobile communication are an almost forgettable part of our day-to-day lives, with criminal usage of either being more of a nuisance than a societal problem. Such technologies are also often used by law enforcement to catch criminals, an ironic shift that we can reasonably expect to eventually happen to blockchains.

A False Image

New technologies are always controversial when they first appear. The public tends to be suspicious of what it doesn't understand, and the people who've benefited from the status quo are afraid of losing their standing. Throw in a handful of attention-grabbing headlines involving shadowy thieves and hackers, and you have the perfect recipe for a bad first impression. It's a story that we've heard many times before, with other new technologies.

The cure is the widespread adoption that always comes for any technology that makes life easier and commerce more efficient. As more and more people see the benefits of using cryptocoins to save, invest, and transact, and as practical smart contracts and dapps change our relationship with software, interacting with a blockchain will eventually become as commonplace as using the Internet is today—more likely to be taken for granted than taken aback by.

To arrive at that future, our laws, regulations, and cultural mores will have to evolve to accommodate this new way of doing things. Nowhere is that truer than with the controversial world of initial coin offerings.

CONSIDER THIS

o In 1988, a *New York Times* headline read "Schools Responding to Beeper, Tool of Today's Drug Dealer, by Banning It."

o In 2013, the *New York Times* columnist and economics Nobel laureate Paul Krugman published a column titled "Bitcoin is Evil."

o Also in 2013, a ZDNet headline read "Bitcoin is going to teach you a lesson. A costly one."

o In 2017, when the price of Bitcoin was below $5,000, Jamie Dimon, the CEO of JPMorgan Chase, called the cryptocurrency a fraud and a bubble, adding "If you were in Venezuela or Ecuador or North Korea or a bunch of parts like that, or if you were a drug dealer, a murderer, stuff like that, you are better off doing it in bitcoin than US dollars. ...so there may be a market for that, but it would be a limited market."

o In 2018, when the price of Bitcoin was above $15,000, Dimon said he regretted making those comments.

15

Initial Coin Offerings

One of the most important components of a successful blockchain is the **network effect**, the business term used to describe services where the value to existing users goes up with each additional user. The more people who sign up to use a social media platform like Facebook or chat program like WhatsApp, the more valuable those services become. Blockchains work the same way.

The simplest definition of an **initial coin offering**, or **ICO**, is *a crowdfunding effort by a blockchain development team that simultaneously funds a new project and creates a network effect for its eventual product or service.*

Startups traditionally get funding by issuing shares to angel investors and venture capital funds via a cumbersome legal process. This also results in a few investors owning most of a company, which can lead to problems down the road. Since blockchains have their own fast and efficient platform for handling digital tokens, and since all blockchain-based projects need to foster a community of users to succeed, most startups in this space prefer going the crowdfunding route. Initial coin offerings allow blockchain startups to easily raise money while creating a user base for their product.

The first prominent ICO was the one used by Ethereum to launch its blockchain. During the initial fundraising window, anyone who submitted bitcoins to the Ethereum Foundation was promised a proportional amount of ether in return. Once the blockchain was launched the following year, every contributor was emailed the private key to an existing address that held their coins.

Funding their project with an ICO allowed Ethereum's developers to avoid the concentration of ownership that usually results from traditional financing. Since ether was designed to be a store of value, means of exchange and the currency in which miners were paid to run smart contracts, starting off with broad participation was vital to the project's success.

Crowdfunding Copycats

Many other ICOs have successfully raised money from blockchain participants in recent years. Some, like The DAO, issued tokens that resembled shares in a business. Others issued tokens that would be a core component of their purpose, like the chips for an online casino or the vouchers for a blockchain-based cloud-storage network.

Coin offerings conducted prior to the existence of Ethereum had to develop their own blockchain. Ethereum's built-in token functionality eliminated that barrier, allowing anyone to issue a new token for any purpose at minimal cost, because their token could just ride the Ethereum blockchain. Just as the World Wide Web and its standardized system of web browsing and URLs helped create the dot-com boom of the 1990s, the arrival of Ethereum launched a digital gold rush.

The first major ICO launched on Ethereum was The DAO. Despite its tragic ending, investors fell in love with the idea of using blockchain technology to invest in new blockchain-based projects, and by the spring of 2017 money started pouring into new offerings. The hype surrounding some of those early projects also led to their tokens trading up in the secondary market once they were issued, creating a virtuous cycle where everyone involved was making money, all with the added benefit of little regulatory scrutiny.

The Race Is On

Most ICOs aim to raise a fixed amount of money during a specific time period and reject any further contributions once their quota is filled. In the summer of 2017, ICOs whose creators expected would take days to complete started hitting their funding targets in minutes, sometimes even seconds, leaving some investors out. The de facto exclusivity that these brief investment windows created led to a sort of arms race among people trying to get into the next hot deal.

Just as with Bitcoin, Ethereum's miners always process the highest-paying transactions first. To make sure that their contribution got in before a popular ICO filled up, investors started paying higher and higher transaction fees along with their contribution to jump the line, crowding out any non-ICO related transactions, and causing the entire network to practically come to a standstill during each offering as miners and nodes struggled to keep up.

The burden that some ICOs placed on Ethereum's blockchain also shed a light on the particulars of how they were being executed. There is no standard way to do an ICO, and each project is free to use its own implementation. In one infamous instance, the smart contract managing a coin offering was so poorly designed that, when combined with the sheer demand for the deal, it practically caused the entire blockchain—not to mention the price of ether—to crash. Critics of the event began calling for greater regulations on new offerings.

Silly Season

Easy money has a tendency to loosen standards, and the ICO boom of 2017 was no exception. The earlier practice of a project's developers first laying a solid foundation before trying to raise money was quickly replaced by so-called vaporware, and the ICO calendar filled up with projects that offered little more than a business plan. Suddenly, every company that had a remote connection to blockchain technology was trying to raise millions, with random celebrities and promoters pushing their favorite offerings on social media.

Due to its historical propensity for booms and busts, the securities industry is one of the most regulated in most countries, especially when it comes to startups. Many countries have accredited investor laws that require startups to take money only from investors who are both sophisticated enough to understand the risks and affluent enough to withstand them. Since blockchains treat all comers equally, and contain no information about individual participants, most ICOs were taking money from anyone.

The inevitable crackdown started in the summer of 2017, when the Securities and Exchange Commission (SEC) put out a ruling that the tokens issued by the infamous DAO of the prior year were in fact securities, and should have followed all U.S. government guidelines on such issuing. Although the regulatory body said they had no plans to prosecute anyone for failing to do so in that instance, the message sent across the blockchain space was clear: ICOs would now be regulated.

Other countries took an even firmer stance. In China and Korea, where ICO participation had been especially popular and the quality of offerings had been particularly bad, regulators banned all initial coin offerings outright.

Apples and Oranges

Blockchain enthusiasts argued that securities regulations should not be applied to blockchain startups, because the coins and tokens they were issuing were different from shares in a traditional company. You can't use your Apple shares to buy an iPhone, and being an angel investor in Uber has nothing to do with taking a cab. Tokens on the other hand, although issued in exchange for investment capital, usually exist to serve a purpose.

Augur uses tokens as a reward for those who help settle the outcome of a bet. Basic Attention Tokens connect advertisers with content creators. Siacoins let you rent space on somebody else's hard drive. Whereas traditional companies issue shares only to raise money, most blockchain companies issue tokens to create a user base.

To make matters even more confusing, public blockchains have no owners, as opposed to traditional corporations. Most blockchain projects only have a foundation or nonprofit body that takes in the proceeds from an ICO and pays programmers and developers. The blockchain itself only exists because a critical mass of voluntary participants find it useful and agree to its rules of operations. There are no certificates of incorporation or tax ID numbers.

The challenge of figuring out how to properly regulate blockchains without stifling their development is a big one. Like everyone else involved in this space, government bodies are going to have to learn to think differently, and new laws are going to have to be passed.

Blockchains represent such a radical shift in the way our society functions that many of the old rules no longer apply, and nowhere is this truer than in the wild world of cryptocoin investing.

CONSIDER THIS

o ICOs surpassed early-round VCs as the biggest source of funding for Internet startups in 2017.

o The biggest ICO in 2016 managed to raise only $16 million. The biggest one in 2017 raised $257 million.

o The fastest ICO recorded to date was the one for the Brave browser, which managed to hit its $35 million fundraising target in just 30 seconds.

o During the peak of the ICO craze, one eager investor paid $1,500 worth of ether in mining fees alone, just to be first in line to have their transaction verified by the miners. The average Ethereum mining fee at that time was less than a dollar.

o Celebrities who publicly endorsed an offering on social media included boxer Floyd Mayweather Jr. and reality star Paris Hilton.

16

Investing

The first time anyone ever used a cryptocoin to actually buy something was in the spring of 2010, when a Florida resident bought two pizzas for 10,000 bitcoins. Had he held on to those coins instead, today their value would be almost $100 million.

Eye-popping investment returns are the norm for anyone who started investing in cryptocoins early in their life cycle. In less than a decade, the combined market cap of all coins

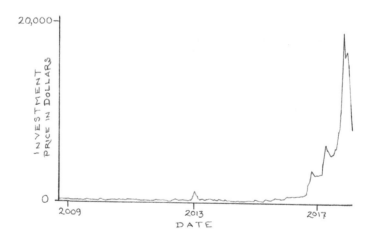

Figure 15. Bitcoin Price Appreciation

and tokens has gone from zero to over $400 billion, a feat only possible with outsized gains, year after year.

The pizza just mentioned wasn't actually paid for in bitcoins, as no businesses accepted cryptocoin payments back then. Instead, one early adopter posted on a message board that he would be willing to do an exchange, and an intrepid speculator took him up on the offer, paying for the pizza in dollars and having it delivered to the seller's house in exchange for coins sent to him via the blockchain. That deal valued bitcoins at less than a penny. Nine months later each coin was worth a dollar, having appreciated by 10,000%.

The pizza transaction made some news in tech circles, and probably led to some people buying bitcoins for the first time. Five dollars' worth of coins purchased around that time would be worth $20,000 just six months later—the cost of a sandwich turning into the value of a new car—as Bitcoin approached $31.

Six months later, Bitcoin was trading at two bucks, having lost 95% of its value.

Markets that go up parabolically come down just as hard, and few markets have had more moon shots and crash landings than cryptocoins. The chart in Figure 15 doesn't do the volatility justice. In the fall of 2013, just five years after Satoshi Nakamoto published his landmark paper, the price of Bitcoin surpassed $1,000. Eighteen months later, it fell below $200. Having been driven up by news of adoption, it was sent back down by the collapse of Mt. Gox.

All the other cryptocoins have followed a similar boom-bust pattern. Ether that was acquired during the Ethereum crowdsale of 2014 cost approximately 30 cents. It climbed to over $20 a few years later when The DAO's crowdfunding seemed like a success, then collapsed by 70% as it turned into a failure. Today the price of a single coin stands at $800, but it has experienced countless rallies and declines along the way, including one famous instance when it temporarily lost 99% of its value at one of the world's biggest exchanges.

The Implications of Violent Price Swings

Some critics have pointed to the volatility of blockchain-based assets as a reason to be suspicious of the entire space, and accusations of pyramid schemes and bubbles are common, especially from veteran investment professionals. Measured by the standards of almost any other market, they have a point. Stocks, bonds, commodities, or real estate seldom have that kind of volatility, and it's usually a bad omen when they do.

But comparing cryptocoin investing to any other kind of investing is pointless, because nothing like this has ever existed before. Even otherwise successful traders have consistently struggled to come up with a coherent cryptocoin investment strategy, partly because the technology is hard to understand, but mostly because there are no historical benchmarks.

Stock, bond, and foreign-exchange trading have been around long enough for investors to come up with reliable valuation metrics, and most people have a general idea of how their moves are impacted by outside factors like the business cycle or economic policy. Cryptocoin investors, by contrast, are always operating in the dark, because their sector hasn't been around long enough for anyone to really understand it as an investment vehicle.

Then there are the logistical issues. Traditional investing has evolved to the point where anyone can open a brokerage account within a day or two, make some purchases, and know that their investment is safe. There is no such security in the crypto space, because the same blockchain technology that empowers digital ownership also allows digital theft. It's no coincidence that some of the biggest price swings in the space have come from exchange hackings, and the alternative strategy of storing your coins yourself has its own headaches, the least of which is the cumbersome process of constantly sending your coins to and from an exchange.

One of the fundamental tenets of investing is the relationship between risk and reward, and no class of investors in recent memory has had to face as much risk as early crypto adopters. Eight years ago, nobody could be sure that blockchain technology would actually work, never mind if the coins it empowered would gain in value. As the technology has slowly gained legitimacy, the market has handsomely rewarded those who were brave enough to face all its headwinds.

Putting a Dollar Value on Disruption

One way to value the investment potential of any new technology is to look at the size of the industry it threatens to disrupt. The value of Tesla and Airbnb might have appreciated a lot in recent years, but their current valuations seem more reasonable in the context of the total size of the global auto and hotel industries.

Similarly, if a potential investor looks at how much the tokens of blockchain-based cloud storage services like Siacoin and Storj have appreciated since inception, they might assume that, at a combined market cap over $1 billion, the coins are grossly overvalued. But that number is relatively small when compared to the valuations investors already place on existing cloud-storage companies like Dropbox. A blockchain enthusiast might even argue that *should* one of the token-based solutions mentioned succeed, the added features would make it even more valuable than the existing non-decentralized and non-distributed options.

If the relative-value argument is to be believed, then no asset in existence today has more potential upside than a trusted form of digital money, because no industry today has a greater market cap than paper money. The total value of all of the paper money in the world combined is estimated to be $90 trillion. If Bitcoin can take just 1% of that market share, then each of its 16.7 million coins in existence will be worth $50,000.

But even if the level of disruption just mentioned does happen, there is no guarantee that it will happen soon, or that the ultimate winner will be Bitcoin. Just as AOL is not a dominant player in the web today, and Blackberry is no longer a big player in the smartphone market, it's possible that some other cryptocoin will eventually dethrone Bitcoin. The ultimate winner might be a different coin in existence today, or one that hasn't been invented yet.

The Relative-Value Approach

Sorting the winners from the losers is up to the market's price discovery mechanism, and there will be plenty of both along the way. As with any investment boom, it's important to remember that markets reward those that take the greatest risks.

In December 2017 two financial exchanges in America launched the trading of Bitcoin futures, financial products that allowed investors to bet on the future price of the cryptocurrency. Both products were designed to settle all bets in dollars. For the first time ever, investors could now get exposure to the space without having to go through a cryptocoin exchange, interact with a blockchain, or use a wallet. It's reasonable to assume that sooner rather than later we will also have access to cryptocoin ETFs, electronically traded funds that let anyone invest in a currency as easily as they can invest in shares of Amazon.

That means we've come a long way from the days when you practically had to write code to get your hands on some bitcoins. But it also means that the biggest percentage returns are probably behind us, because markets also reward those that overcome the greatest obstacles. The more mature a cryptocoin becomes, the more muted its future investment return. Brave speculators try to game this process, hoping to catch the next hot coin or token before it goes mainstream.

Put On Your Seatbelt

The most popular word in cryptocoin investing is the call to HODL, both an anagram of *hold* and an acronym that stands for "hold on for dear life." Grizzled veterans of this world understand that extreme volatility is a given. Although some try to time the machinations back and forth, most prefer to just ride the wave. Given the extreme levels of volatility and uncertainty, the only investment thesis that makes sense is to proceed with extreme caution, keeping your overall portfolio exposure to this space small, and expecting violent price swings in both directions.

The history of investing in technological revolutions teaches us that first a new technology appears, then an investment bubble forms around it. It's usually not until after that bubble bursts that the technology takes over. How it goes about doing so is what remains to be seen, on the road ahead.

○───○

CONSIDER THIS

○ In June of 2017, the price of ether on the GDAX exchange momentarily crashed from $317 down to 10 *cents,* then rebounded back up. The move was later determined to be caused by a massive market sell order that then triggered sitting stop-loss orders at lower prices.

o In late 2017, the price of Bitcoin rallied significantly on the news that futures on the cryptocurrency would be launched, practically tripling from around $7,000 to almost $20,000 in the weeks between when the financial product was first announced and when it finally began trading. It marked an all-time high on the very first day of futures trading, then lost half its value in the following month.

o In late 2017, the price of Ripple appreciated tenfold, from below 30 cents to over $3, in a matter of weeks as the company announced a series of new partnerships, making the business more valuable than the vast majority of stocks in the S&P 500. In the ensuing two weeks, it lost 75% of its value.

o One of the more prominent investors in Bitcoin are the Winklevoss twins of Facebook fame. They reportedly purchased $13 million in bitcoins back in 2013, and supposedly have held on to all of them, possibly making them Bitcoin billionaires. In 2015 they launched their own cryptocoin exchange, and are also trying to get SEC approval for the first Bitcoin ETF.

17

The Road Ahead

I f you make a list of all the things that our society considers valuable, and rank them by the value they've been accorded, you'll notice something interesting: Most of the items at the top are virtual, existing primarily in our collective imaginations.

APPROXIMATE VALUE IN DOLLARS	
BONDS	$215 TRILLION
FLAT CURRENCIES	$90 TRILLION
STOCKS	$80 TRILLION
OIL CONSUMED IN A YEAR	$2.3 TRILLION
WHEAT GROWN IN A YEAR	$138 BILLION

Figure 16. Dollar Value of Virtual Objects

First on the list is the amount of debt we owe each other, trillions of dollars in bonds that are nothing more than agreements that one entity will someday pay back another. Next is the world's collection of fiat currencies, trillions more that is backed by nothing more than a promise. If aliens came down to Earth tomorrow, they might be wondering what all the fuss is about because so much of what we consider valuable has little to do with what we need to survive, like basic food and shelter. And yet, the dollar value of a single bank might be greater than that of the planet's entire wheat crop.

At some point during our social evolution, we realized that it's beneficial to ascribe value to virtual objects, because doing so creates trust. Strangers that don't have a shared history or common language might have little reason to trust each other, but so long as they trust the same kind of money, they can still work and trade with each other.

Maintaining Trust

That sort of trust is the foundation of our modern society, and a requirement for any economically productive endeavor. A pharmaceutical company will spend billions researching a drug because it trusts that a patent—another virtual object— will protect its ability to earn a return on its investment. A movie studio will invest in a film because it trusts that it will own the rights to it. You will save your money in a certain currency because you trust that its value will hold up.

Trust is never perfect, and there are always those who try to get ahead by cheating the system. Until now, the only way to maintain the integrity of virtual objects was with the help of an intermediary: central banks, courts, patent offices, stock exchanges, record labels, ridesharing companies, Airbnb, casinos, clearinghouses, banks, brokers, and on and on. All of these middlemen provide a vital service, without which civilization could never have gotten this far.

But those same middlemen are not without their flaws, the most obvious of which is the added cost they impose on everything. StubHub, the secondary market for tickets to concerts and sporting events, charges fees that can add up to 25% of the price of the ticket. Given all the work and money it takes to put on a show, it's a bit shocking that a ticketing service can capture a quarter of the total value—a testament both to how much consumers value trust in the ticket market, and why it's important to find a better way.

The Great Disintermediary

To understand how blockchain technology will shape our future, it helps to create a different list. Think of all of the industries where trust is a needed component—and an intermediary charges a costly fee to provide it. Those are the first places where the middleman will be replaced by a decentralized ledger governed by consensus.

Event ticketing is a perfect example because, other than ensuring that buyers get a real ticket and sellers get paid, there's not much else for the intermediary to do. Every ticket is nothing more than a virtual token that gives its owner the right to attend an event. Tracking ownership of that token is the kind of problem blockchains were invented for, which is why multiple such projects are already underway, some creating their own blockchains and others relying on Ethereum.

Enterprise Solutions

Businesses tend to be reliable early adopters, as it's easier to change the culture of a company than that of an entire society. Just as email and cell phones went mainstream on Wall Street long before they did on Main Street, so will blockchain technology. Despite the constant chorus of criticism from bankers directed against cryptocoins, there's universal agreement that the underlying technology will revolutionize the nuts and bolts of finance, too much of which relies on ancient technology.

The earliest changes will take place behind the scenes, which is good, because that's where the infrastructure is most in need of an upgrade. In the spring of 2017, the blockchain community had a good chuckle when the Securities and Exchange Commission (SEC) announced that it was shortening the time it takes for stock and bond transactions to settle—to two *days*. It's not hard to envision a blockchain that would accomplish the same task in two minutes, with more transparency and reliability than ever before.

Although much of the attention in this space goes to public blockchains like Ethereum, a lot of the work being done by developers is on private blockchains that serve specific functions for niche industries, like online advertising or international shipping. Since every blockchain needs a minimum amount of network effect to be viable, a lot of that work is being done by large consortia.

In finance, the R3 consortium of banks and other financial firms is leading the development of the sort of back-office blockchains just mentioned. Looking beyond the financial sector, the Linux Foundation has created Hyperledger, which is developing open-source tools to support a range of industries deploying their own blockchains. The Enterprise Ethereum Alliance, which consists of not only corporations but also academics and researchers, is working on standardizing the creation of smart contracts.

A Messy Transition

While some of the earliest projects to succeed will be niche and private, there will be no shortage of public blockchains designed to improve our day-to-day interactions. The history of innovation teaches us to expect the transition to be anything but smooth and, at least at the outset, to expect more failures than successes.

Public chains have several key obstacles that they need to overcome, the first of which is a lack of quality infrastructure. The hackings, attacks, thefts, and forks of the past few years demonstrate that we are still years away from having platforms that are secure and stable enough for people to trust incorporating into everyday life.

Then, there is the lack of experienced talent. The first blockchain was invented less than 10 years ago, so there are very few seasoned veterans. Most of the entrepreneurs, researchers, and developers currently entering the field come to it from an area that's only tangentially related and will need time to learn, often by making mistakes.

Another challenge is the lack of any proper legal and regulatory framework. Blockchains have the potential to revolutionize our financial economy, but our laws must be updated to accommodate this shift. Until then, there are countless questions to which nobody has an answer: What is the legal status of a decentralized autonomous organization (DAO)? How much privacy will a cryptocurrency be allowed to have? What does the IRS consider the cost basis of a coin born out of a fork? Can a developer be held liable for a faulty smart contract?

Change Will Come, Slowly

Technological revolutions tend to distort our perception of time. Some aspects of our lives change seemingly overnight, while others take forever. The first-ever email was sent almost 50 years ago, and today, your email address is a de facto form of ID. Despite this, there are still large companies that will consider a faxed document official, but not an emailed one.

Technologically speaking, a fax and an email are effectively the same thing—a reproduction of an existing document that is the result of electronic communication—with the slight difference that faxes always result in a piece of paper, while emails usually don't. Our society is so anchored to the belief that only paper documents are official, that all these years later some of us still refuse to fully embrace the better option, despite the fact that an email can always be printed.

The first public blockchains to go mainstream will be affected by the same cultural inertia. To deal with that resistance, they will probably take a new way of doing things and try to make it *look* old. Tokenized dollars transferred on a blockchain, for example, will probably go mainstream long before cryptocoins do, and the first dapps will do everything they can to look like familiar software.

But then, perhaps a slow pace of progress is the best way forward for this revolution, because it can impact so much of what is fundamental to our society: trust, value, and power. Some people will embrace blockchain's progress wholeheartedly, while others will always be suspicious. Some countries will quickly evolve their legal systems to accommodate, while others won't budge. Some industries will embrace the benefits of this new technology, while others will be eliminated by it. Startups will use the technology to take market share, and incumbents will do everything they can to slow them down, up to and including acquiring them.

But the changes will eventually come, because contrary to what some people believe, human beings are always looking for a better reason to trust each other, and blockchain technology is the best reason yet. Between now and then, there will be many booms and busts, crashes and crises, hucksters, hackers, and heroes. All part of the ever-unfolding story of the blockchain, the technology that only a few people understand, but will eventually change everything.

Afterword

The story that you just read is only the first act of this revolution. Now that you have a good grasp of the fundamentals of this world, I invite you to join me on my website, where I will regularly post a more in-depth analysis of various aspects of the blockchain space. In the months and years to come, I will be discussing everything from philosophical questions to investment considerations.

You can also sign up for my mailing list, which will be the primary means through which I reach out to readers.

www.omidmalekan.com

Until then, I encourage you to use the following tutorial to experience cryptocurrency transactions for yourself.

A Simple Tutorial for Your First Cryptocoin Transactions

Understanding how blockchain technology and cryptocoins work requires a new kind of thinking, and the best way to develop that thinking is by interacting with the technology. The following tutorial will walk you through the basics of acquiring a cryptocoin, moving it through the blockchain, storing it, and ultimately exchanging it for another coin. We are going to deal with ether for this tutorial for the simple reason that it's the most liquid and widely available cryptocurrency that can still be transacted relatively cheaply.

It's natural to be anxious about doing your first cryptocoin transaction. Most people are. That's why it's best to start with a very small amount first. The experience that you gain is independent of the value at stake, and most blockchains accept transactions in small fractions, so you can deal with more expensive coins while keeping your overall exposure small.

Before you can start learning about this world, you have to unlearn some of what you already know about how money moves. Blockchains give digital items physical properties, which means that mistakes that would pose an inconvenience

in traditional banking can be downright catastrophic in cryptocurrencies. There are no replaced debit cards or stopped
checks in this world. The following rules will help you avoid
some of the most common mistakes.

The Crypto Commandments

I. **Always keep your private key private and secure.**
   Whoever possesses the private key to a blockchain address,
   owns its content.

II. **Practice protective redundancy.**
   All of the information pertaining to a blockchain address,
   including its private key, wallet password, and pin code,
   should be stored in at least one, but preferably two, alternate and secure locations before any funds are sent to that
   address.

III. **Make sure you can get money out before
   putting a significant amount in.**
   Anytime you are using a new blockchain address or wallet, deposit a tiny amount into it, then make sure you can
   withdraw the funds before sending larger amounts there.

IV. **Always do a small test transaction first.**
   Before doing any transaction on a blockchain, whether it's
   sending or receiving coins, confirm that you have the right
   information by transacting a small percentage of the total
   amount.

v. Obscurity is the best security.

Thieves can't steal what they don't know you own. Avoid publicizing your account on social media or anywhere else.

STEP 1: Acquire Ether

The best way to initially get your hands on some ether is to have a friend who owns some send you a tiny amount. If that's not an option, you can also buy some at a centralized exchange that allows people to buy cryptocoins with a fiat currency. Which exchange you should use depends on where you live and what currency you'd like to deposit. Sites like CoinMarketCap (www.coinmarketcap.com) can show you where a specific coin trades. To see such a list for ether, go to the site's homepage, click on "Ethereum" and select the "Markets" tab. Make sure you pick an exchange that trades ether against the fiat currency you'll be depositing. Many cryptocoin exchanges do not accept fiat deposits and only offer trading of one coin for another.

The same coins will often trade at slightly different prices on different exchanges. This has nothing to do with the blockchain, which treats all coins as the same, and is caused by different supply and demand dynamics at different exchanges in different countries. During periods of extreme market volatility, price discrepancies from one exchange to another can be quite large. But since we are sticking to very small amounts for this tutorial, such discrepancies don't matter.

Once you've opened an exchange account and funded it, you can go ahead and purchase a small amount of ether. At this point the exchange will show you as the "owner" of the cryptocoin, but that is only an illusion. In the blockchain universe, you don't truly own a coin until it resides on an address for which you control the private key. Coins on exchanges are held in the exchanges' blockchain address. All you see when they show you your balance is an IOU. To take full possession of your ether, you'll need to withdraw it from the exchange and have them send it to your address via the blockchain. To do that, you'll need to install a wallet.

STEP 2: Install a Wallet

Cryptocoin wallets come in many varieties. Anything that has the ability to store a bit of information can be considered a wallet, including a piece of paper where you write down your blockchain address and private key. Many users consider this so-called **paper wallet** the safest way to store coins, as long as there are redundant copies stored in multiple secure locations. The downside to paper wallets is that, each time you want to move money from your account, you have to manually enter your private key into some software that can communicate with the blockchain. Since the purpose of this tutorial is to practice transacting, we'll use a more convenient method.

Several for-profit companies make small devices called **hardware wallets**. Such devices store your public address and private key, and have many built-in security features, the biggest one of which being the fact that, like paper wallets, they are considered **cold storage**, blockchain slang for storing your private key using a method that doesn't regularly expose it to the Internet. Hardware wallets can be expensive, but given their combination of security and usability, they are considered the best way to store and transact large sums of cryptocoins.

For the purposes of this tutorial, we are going to use a **software wallet**, *a program that runs on a computer or smartphone and stores your public address and private key.* While this type of wallet is less secure than a hardware or paper wallet, it is much more convenient and easier to use. For our example, we are going to use MyEtherWallet, or MEW (www .myetherwallet.com), a popular and free Ethereum wallet that stores your address and private key on your own computer and uses a web browser to interact with the blockchain.

To begin, go to www.myetherwallet.com and click "New Wallet" at the top. The first thing the site will do is prompt you to create a new password. Note that this password is not your private key, but rather an added layer of security where MEW uses the password to encrypt the private key it stores on your computer, protecting it from viruses and malware. This is their way of practicing the first crypto commandment.

Next, MEW will prompt you to download and save a keystore file. This file contains your private key, encrypted by the password you just created. Its purpose is to help you fulfill the second crypto commandment by backing up your private key in an alternate location. The best place to store this file is on a device that is not ordinarily connected to the Internet, like a USB drive. Such a device is best stored somewhere secure and far from the computer where you install MEW, in case of a fire or flood.

In the next step, MEW will show you your actual private key and ask you to print it out to put in a paper wallet. This is an added form of redundancy in case you lose your keystore file, or forget the password that unlocks it. You need to be very careful with this information. Never store an unencrypted private key in the cloud, on your phone, or in an email, and never expose it in public.

Next, MEW will offer to finally show you your public address, but before doing so, it will make sure you can reload your keystore file and have the right password for it. This complies with the third crypto commandment. Select the option to move forward via "Keystore/JSON File" and upload the file you just downloaded, then enter your MEW password.

If you see the message "Wallet Successfully Decrypted," it means that you've properly reloaded your keystore and recalled your password. (If you see an error message, it means you likely made a mistake at some point along the way, and need to start the process over.)

At this point, you should be able to see your Ethereum address. You can identify it by the fact that it starts with 0x, as all Ethereum addresses do. This is your public address, which you can share with anyone who wants to send you ether. MEW will also show you a QR code for your address. Many cryptocoin transactions are done using software wallets on smartphones that can use the camera to scan the QR code. This is only an added convenience, as you could always just copy and paste the text of your address.

STEP 3: Make Your First Blockchain Transaction

Now you are ready to send your coins from the exchange where you purchased them to your personal blockchain address. Go through your exchange's withdrawal process, and enter your new Ethereum address. Per the fourth crypto commandment, you should try withdrawing a small percentage of your balance first.

Some exchanges release withdrawals immediately, while others can take minutes or even hours. Your MEW wallet should reflect the transaction as soon as your exchange broadcasts it on the Internet, but given the Ethereum blockchain's transparency, you can also track it on a third-party website. Looking up information using a blockchain explorer is an important skill to learn.

Go to Etherscan's website (etherscan.io), then copy and paste your Ethereum address from MEW into that site's search field. If your exchange has already sent your coins, you should be able to see the transaction on the blockchain, along with the time it was initiated and the number of block confirmations it has thus far. You can also see the transaction's unique TxHash, or ID number. That really long string of letters and numbers will forever be the way to identify this particular transaction. Another way to see it will be by looking up the transaction history of this particular address.

Don't worry if you see the transaction on the blockchain explorer but not in your wallet. Wallets can sometimes lag during periods of peak activity. Since every transaction is nothing more than an entry in the ledger, so long as the blockchain shows a coin balance in an address for which you control the private key, you are the owner of those coins, regardless of what your wallet says.

Once you are satisfied that your small test transaction has worked and that you have all of the right information, go ahead and send the rest of your exchange balance to your wallet address.

STEP 4: Prepare to Exchange Cryptocurrencies

Exchanging one type of coin for another is an important part of using blockchain technology. For this tutorial, we are going to exchange some of your ether for Bitcoin Cash, so you can also experience what a Bitcoin transaction looks like, while avoiding the high fees that currently make small transactions on the original Bitcoin blockchain unfeasible.

Since MEW only handles Ethereum transactions, we are going to install a new wallet called Jaxx (jaxx.io) to store Bitcoin Cash. Jaxx is a free multicoin wallet with a friendly user interface that can be installed on a mobile device or computer. Go to the Jaxx website to download and install the software. Be aware that unlike MEW, Jaxx does not encrypt the private key it stores on your computer, making it vulnerable to viruses and malware. Never store significant sums of cryptocoins in a wallet like Jaxx.

After you launch Jaxx for the first time, pick "Create New Wallet" and select "Express Setup." Check off Bitcoin Cash as the currency you'd like to use, then hit "Take Me To My Wallet." Jaxx will immediately initialize your wallet and reveal your new Bitcoin Cash address on the blockchain. But before doing the exchange, you need to once again practice the crypto commandments and backup your private key.

Go to "Menu" and then "Tools." Here you can just request Jaxx show you your private key, but to see a different backup option, select "Backup Wallet," and on the next menu, select "Backup Wallet" again. This will guide you through the process of writing down a backup phrase.

Backup phrases, which are known as **mnemonic seeds**, were invented to help users back up and restore their wallets more easily. Since private keys are notoriously hard to write down and type back in, a random combination of words, presented in a specific order, is instead used by the wallet to generate your private key. That unique combination of words will always generate the same private key, with the added convenience that the same seed can be used across multiple blockchains. All of the different cryptocoins that Jaxx supports can be backed up with just one seed. The mnemonic also makes it easy to duplicate or move your wallet, for example, from your computer to your mobile device. All you would have to do is install Jaxx elsewhere and type in your phrase. But remember, your mnemonic, just like your private key, should always be kept secure and hidden.

Once you've practiced the commandments by saving and then reentering your seed, you are ready to receive some bitcoin cash.

STEP 5: Exchange One Coin for Another

Exchanging ether for bitcoin cash can be done at any centralized or decentralized exchange that handles both coins. For this tutorial, we are going to use a hybrid service called ShapeShift (shapeshift.io), a for-profit company that allows you to anonymously exchange one coin for another without having to register an account.

Go to shapeshift.io and select Ether in the "Deposit" field and Bitcoin Cash in the "Receive" field, then pick the "Quick" option and click "Continue." ShapeShift will then show you their current exchange rate, along with the maximum and minimum amount they will transact. Copy and paste your Bitcoin Cash address from Jaxx into the top box, and then your Ethereum address from MEW into the bottom one. (The Ethereum address will only be used if something goes wrong and ShapeShift needs to refund the ether you send them.) After reading their terms, check the box that you agree and click "Start Transaction."

ShapeShift will now tell you where to send your ether. This new address was generated by the service specifically for the purpose of your exchange, so any coins that show up in it will be credited toward your Bitcoin Cash purchase. After confirming that they have your correct info, including your Ethereum refund address and your Bitcoin Cash address, copy the address under "Send to this address."

Now, open your MEW wallet. This time, click on "Send Ether & Tokens" in MEW and follow their instructions for uploading your keystore file and entering your password. Now you can paste the address you copied from ShapeShift into MEW's "To Address" and also type in the amount you wish to send. Make sure that amount is within ShapeShift's stated range, and click "Generate Transaction," then "Send Transaction." Use MEW's confirmation screen to confirm that you have the right address from ShapeShift, then click "Yes, I am sure! Make transaction."

The rest of this process is entirely automated. The Shape-Shift website will update with each step, first reflecting the fact that they received your transmission via the Ethereum blockchain, and lastly confirming that your Bitcoin Cash was sent via its blockchain. Once this happens, click "See it on the blockchain" to experience using the Bitcoin Cash blockchain explorer. Your balance should also show up in your Jaxx wallet.

Congratulations, you have now purchased a coin using fiat money, stored it in a wallet, and exchanged it for another coin. Practice is an important part of learning how this world works, so it is highly recommended that you do many more of these types of transactions using insignificant sums to learn. Now that you've installed Jaxx, you can initiate other coins on it and use ShapeShift to purchase them as well. Mistakes are bound to happen, but a mistake made with an insignificant amount of money now will teach you an important lesson for when you start moving more-significant funds later.

CONSIDER THIS

○ In 2013, a Bloomberg reporter doing a story on Bitcoin for Bloomberg TV gave one of the show's anchors
a paper wallet with $20 worth of Bitcoin as a gift live
on the air. The anchor momentarily exposed the private key to the camera, leading to the funds being
stolen by an intrepid viewer shortly thereafter.

○ MEW's software is designed so the creators of the
wallet never see your private key, but services like
it are popular targets of phishing attacks, when a
malicious user sends you a fake link to a website
that looks like the wallet service, but is in fact a
facade designed to trick you into exposing your private key.

○ Seed mnemonics allow for another feature common
in cryptocoin wallets, hierarchical deterministic
(HD) addresses. Wallets that support that feature,
like Jaxx, let you generate an infinite number of new
public addresses, without having to back up a new
private key each time. Every new address is still generated from the same seed. This feature gives you
the ability to transact more anonymously, as you can
always generate a new address for each transaction.

o The thief who stole the Bloomberg anchor's coins
  was a member of the blockchain community who
  wanted to use the opportunity to teach everyone
  an important lesson about protecting one's private
  key. As soon as he stole the funds, he contacted his
  victim and offered to return them right away, in
  exchange for another TV report on the importance
  of being careful with cryptocoins. The anchor was so
  impressed by that gesture that he decided to let the
  thief keep the money.

Alt Coin Appendix

ETHEREUM
Native currency ETH

It is a testament to Ethereum's smart contract usability and potential that, despite being one of the newer projects in the industry (having only been launched in mid-2015), it still boasts the second-highest market cap. The price of ETH skyrocketed in 2017 after a myriad of independent projects were launched on it, including hundreds of initial coin offerings (ICOs). Ethereum's inherent token-creation functionality is so easy to use that many startups decided to forego the costly and time-consuming process of launching their own cryptocoin and blockchain and instead just issue a new token on Ethereum.

The Enterprise Ethereum Alliance, a consortium of some of the world's biggest companies, is currently exploring how it might use the platform, or a private version of it, to revolutionize the way countless industries operate.

Unlike the highly fragmented Bitcoin community, Ethereum currently has a unified development team led by its founder, and has a clear future roadmap to deal with issues of security and scalability. (See Chapters 5 through 8 for more on Ethereum.)

RIPPLE
Native currency XRP

Whereas Bitcoin was invented to replace our existing financial system, Ripple's mission is to help improve it. Its founders believe that what's wrong with our current way of doing things is not paper money or the banking system, but rather the aging infrastructure that today's banks use to transact with each other.

The Ripple network allows banks to quickly and securely send and receive any financial asset, be it dollars, stocks, or even Bitcoins, across borders and around the world. A blockchain similar to that of Bitcoin facilitates these interbank transactions with the implementation of a distributed ledger, one that not only keeps track of every asset passed through it but also its native currency, which banks using the network have to buy and use to pay for access. Because Ripple is designed primarily for speed, it boasts one of the fastest block times of any blockchain, completing a new block every few seconds.

The development team that invented and currently manages the Ripple network believes that once banks have a faster and cheaper way of transacting with each other they can offer faster and cheaper transactions to their clients, avoiding the need to create an entirely new financial system.

It's worth noting that the Ripple network is much more centralized than most popular cryptocoin blockchains, and that the for-profit company that manages the network still owns the vast majority of Ripple tokens. For these reasons, some blockchain enthusiasts do not consider XRP to be a true cryptocoin.

LITECOIN
Native currency LTC

Litecoin was invented in 2011 by a Google engineer named Charles Lee who set out to improve the speed by which a blockchain handled financial transactions. He started out by copying much of the Bitcoin blockchain's rules of operation, then made several key changes to its mining algorithm to speed things up.

All currencies are both stores of value and mediums of exchange, but each can be more of one than the other. Lee has described Litecoin as the silver to Bitcoin's gold, offering a bit less security in exchange for a lot more usability. The Litecoin blockchain averages a new block every two and a half minutes—four times faster than Bitcoin. It also boasts a faster inflation schedule than Bitcoin, and the total number of Litecoins that will ever be mined is four times larger than Bitcoin as well, making the junior currency less scarce for savers but more available for those wanting to use it to pay for purchases.

LTC has often been the beneficiary of the Bitcoin scaling debate, both in terms of attention and price appreciation. Like Ethereum, it has a tight group of developers whose proposals are accepted by the larger blockchain community without much controversy. Thanks to its founding mission to make cryptocoin transactions faster, and its own implementation of the Segregated Witness (SegWit) technology upgrade, Litecoin is on its way to be one of the first major blockchains to to implement the Lightning Network, the leading concept for a peripheral transaction network that operates far faster than any existing blockchain.

DASH
Native currency DASH

Dash is another blockchain project meant to allow decentralized, fast and cheap transactions using a native cryptocoin. It distinguishes itself from predecessors like Bitcoin and Litecoin with its governance structure. If those other blockchains are viewed as pure democracies, where anyone can choose to be a miner or node and have a say in proposed upgrades, Dash's blockchain is more like a republic, one in which masternodes are empowered to make key decisions.

To become a masternode, a participant must first put 1,000 Dash coins in escrow with the blockchain. Doing so allows them to not only store a copy of the blockchain, but also to have an important vote in future upgrades as well as process special transactions. Unlike most other blockchains, masternodes in Dash get paid for helping maintain and improve the network. Whereas the Bitcoin, Ethereum, and Litecoin blockchains only distribute new coins to miners, the Dash mining algorithm reserves almost half of the new coins created by each block for the masternodes as compensation.

Like Litecoin, Dash boasts average block times that are four times faster than Bitcoin, and in 2016 its masternodes voted to scale up by adopting a larger block size, with little fanfare.

MONERO
Native currency XMR

The Bitcoin blockchain is private in that participants are identified by their public addresses instead of their names, but that's not the same as anonymous. If a user's public address is revealed by someone who has transacted with them before, or by accident, then all of their past transaction activity becomes public. Monero is the leading blockchain solution to this problem, offering users full anonymity, both of their identity and transaction history.

Monero, and other blockchains like it, rely on advanced forms of cryptography that allow two parties to agree on the validity of a container of information without knowing what's inside it. Every Monero transaction is put into an information blender that takes the different properties of multiple transactions (like sender, recipient, and number of coins) and mixes them all together. That way, even if a user's Monero address is made public, it's almost impossible to decipher their transaction history. If a Monero user wants to disclose their transaction history to a specific individual, they can provide them with an additional key that will unlock such information.

Monero first gained prominence in 2016 when one of the Internet's leading underground websites for buying drugs and other illicit activities announced its adoption due to its privacy features. Critics of cryptocoins like Monero claim that they help criminals avoid detection, and the FBI has singled it out as a cryptocoin it is concerned about.

NEO
Native currencies NEO and GAS

The universally recognized power of smart contracts in general and the success of Ethereum specifically have led to the creation of other blockchain-based platforms that can handle both cryptocoin transactions and programming instructions. Chinese-based NEO is one of the most valuable.

NEO is similar to Ethereum in that it allows for the issuance of tokens and the development of dapps. But unlike Ethereum, which can only be programmed in its own programming language, NEO smart contracts can be built using existing languages like C# and Java. Also unlike Ethereum, which uses the same native currency both as a means of exchange and to pay the blockchain to run smart contracts, the NEO blockchain has two different coins for each purpose. Its native currency, NEO, is generated as a reward to miners in every block. Its other currency, called GAS, is generated as a sort of interest to anyone holding NEO, and is required to pay the network to process smart contracts.

Some blockchain enthusiasts believe the strongest argument in favor of NEO is its Chinese roots. The communist party in China has a long history of banning foreign online services like Facebook and YouTube and instead promoting homegrown versions that allow for greater censorship and control by the government. After a strong crackdown on all domestic cryptocoin investing by the government in the fall of 2017, some believe that NEO is the leading candidate to be the first officially sanctioned blockchain in China.

TETHER
Native currency USDT

Although blockchains were initially invented to facilitate the transaction of cryptocoins and other digital assets, the simplest use case for a distributed and decentralized ledger is the tracking and movement of existing currencies. Tether provides this service for the U.S. dollar.

The company digitizes dollars by depositing them at a bank, then issuing blockchain-based USDT tokens for each on a one-to-one basis. Those tokens can then be transacted on a blockchain. Users can find security in the fact that they could always send their tokens back to the company in exchange for a check or wire of the dollars they represent.

USDT is popular among blockchain enthusiasts who don't want to deal with the volatility of cryptocurrencies like Bitcoin. Many crypto exchanges that allow for the trading of one cryptocurrency for another have adopted USDT as a proxy for dollars, so their users can still convert cryptocoins to dollars and vice versa without the exchange having to tie into the existing banking system.

Although tokenized paper money like USDT can offer some of the benefits of a cryptocoin, it is not as secure as a completely decentralized and algorithmic coin like Bitcoin. Both Tether and the traditional bank where it stores the dollars backing each token represent centralized points of potential failure, as became apparent in early 2017, when banking problems temporarily drove the value of USDT down to 93 cents on the dollar.

IOTA
Native currency MIOTA

IOTA is a decentralized platform designed for the facilitation of the Internet of things. As more and more household and commercial electronic devices like refrigerators and smart thermostats become connected to the Internet, there is a growing need for a fast and trustworthy network to handle all the data and communication such devices require.

Although the IOTA network is also based on a distributed ledger that nobody owns, its technically different from other blockchains, because it doesn't have any blocks. The Internet of things will eventually include billions of devices that are constantly talking to each other, creating a data load that no traditional blockchain, however fast, could handle.

The IOTA network is designed to deliver almost instantaneous and free transactions by turning every user into a verifier. Before a device can use the network to send out information or a transaction, it must first verify two random transactions for other devices. Theoretically speaking, a smart thermostat can verify the milk order of a smart refrigerator before transmitting its own data. Since every network participant must always verify more transactions than they initiate, the network is said to be infinitely scalable.

IOTA's native currency is different from that of other blockchains, because users don't have to use it to participate in the network. Its only purpose is to serve as the in-network currency for devices that also need to send money.

AUGUR
Native token REP

Augur is a decentralized prediction market and one of the first major dapps to be launched on Ethereum. Prediction markets are places where individuals can bet on the outcome of important events like elections, and have historically shown to be better at predicting outcomes than polls or individual experts.

Augur is a platform through which anyone can launch Ethereum-based smart contracts that allow for rule-based betting on specific outcomes. Bets are placed using Ethereum's native currency, and winners are paid in ether as well.

Augur's native Reputation token, often referred to as REP, exists to facilitate the process of picking winners. Centralized decision markets rely on an individual or a preselected group of individuals to declare the winner of a bet, creating a potential point of corruption. Augur's smart contracts on the other hand crowdsource the settlement process, allowing anyone that owns REP to vote on the winner. Those that vote with the majority are granted more REP, while those that go against are penalized.

STEEMIT
Native currencies STEEM, STEEM POWER, STEEM DOLLARS

Steemit is the most valuable of a series of blockchain projects whose goal is to liberate user-created content that exists on social media sites and web forums and create a platform where the users, instead of the hosts, make money. Its creators argue that it doesn't make sense for creators of popular content to upload their work to sites like Reddit and Facebook where someone else gets to collect the resulting ad revenues.

The Steemit platform rewards both content creators and curators with new coins created by its blockchain. Creators who write the content with the most upvotes, as well those curators who upvote content that ends up becoming popular, get compensated for their efforts with their native currency. All of the user-generated content is also stored on the block-chain, providing added security and decentralization.

Steemit's actual implementation of this idea is rather complicated, but many blockchain enthusiasts believe that it's only a matter of time until the disintermediating force of the block-chain replaces today's highly profitable content gatekeepers with communities where readers pay money into some kind of pool managed by a blockchain that compensates those that submit the most popular content.

Glossary

ADDRESS: a specific account on a blockchain.

ALT COIN: a cryptocurrency other than Bitcoin.

BITCOIN: a cryptocurrency invented by an anonymous developer with a fixed inflation schedule and using a proof-of-work consensus mechanism.

BLOCK: a batch of transactions entered into the ledger at the same time.

BLOCKCHAIN: a technology that allows for something digital to exist in only one place.

COLD STORAGE: a method of storing one's private key that doesn't ordinarily expose it to the Internet.

CONFIRMATIONS: the number of blocks mined so far that have validated a transaction.

CRYPTOCOIN: a unit of cryptocurrency.

CRYPTOCOIN EXCHANGE: a business that facilitates buyers and sellers coming together to trade cryptocoins against each other or against paper forms of money. **Centralized** versions allow users to store their coins at the exchange, while **decentralized** versions only facilitate transactions through the blockchain.

CRYPTOCURRENCY: a purely electronic form of money designed to take advantage of the distributed, decentralized and trust-building nature of a blockchain.

DAO: a decentralized autonomous organization, or programmed entity that exists in the jurisdiction of a blockchain, issues tokens to stakeholders, and fulfills functions governed by smart contracts.

DAPP: open-source and distributed program residing on a block-chain that performs a specific function.

DIFFICULTY: the average amount of computational work it takes to solve the math puzzle before a new block can be mined.

FORK: a change at a specific block of a blockchain that creates an alternate version of history.

GAS: the amount of Ether a smart contract or dapp user must pay the miners on Ethereum to process their usage.

HARD FORK: a change to the consensus rules of a blockchain where the rules that govern its transactions are grown to be more accepting going forward.

HARDWARE WALLET: a physical device built by a manufacturer for the specific purpose of storing cryptocoins and interacting with the blockchain.

HASH POWER: the amount of computing power available to solve the math puzzle and process new transactions at any given point in time.

HIERACHIAL DERTERMINISTIC: a type of blockchain where a mnemonic seed can be used to generate a private key, and mulitple publich addresses can be generated from the same key.

ICO: or initial coin offering, a crowdfunding effort by a block-chain development team that simultaneously funds a new project and creates a network effect for its eventual product or service.

INFLATION SCHEDULE: the mathematical formula that deter-mines when the consensus mechanism of a cryptocurrency gen-erates new coins and determines how many will be created.

MARKET CAP: or market capitalization, a method of determining the total value of a cryptocurrency by taking the number of cryp-tocoins in circulation and multiplying by the value of each coin.

MINERS: entities that process and write the latest batch of trans-actions into the ledger.

MNEMONIC SEED: a random list of words used to generate a private key, for easier backup and recovery.

MONEY: a socially agreed upon store of value, unit of account, and means of exchange.

NETWORK EFFECT: a service where the value to each existing user goes up with every new user.

NODES: entities that store existing copies of the ledger.

OPEN SOURCE: a category of software that has a design and implementation that are transparent to the public.

ORPHANED: a block that is abandoned by the rest of the chain via the consensus mechanism.

PAPER WALLET: a simple way of storing and accessing crypto-coins that relies on writing the corresponding blockchain address and private key on a piece of paper.

PRIVATE KEY: a long string of letters and numbers that can be used to access the contents of a blockchain address.

PROOF OF WORK: a consensus mechanism for writing a blockchain that requires miners to do computational work before being granted the right to write the next block.

PROOF OF STAKE: a consensus mechanism for writing a blockchain that requires a miner to put coins at stake before being granted the right to write the next block.

REDUNDANCY: a backup mechanism used to make sure that vital systems are always operational.

SMART CONTRACT: an agreement between different parties, executed in real time on a blockchain, in a manner that is guaranteed to satisfy all those who agreed to its terms.

SOFT FORK: a change to the consensus rules of a blockchain where the set of rules governing its transactions are shaved to be more limiting going forward.

TOKENS: a new cryptocurrency created on a smart contract platform like Ethereum.

WALLET: software or hardware that stores your address and private key and interacts with the blockchain on your behalf.

About the Author

Omid Malekan has been involved in the blockchain space as an investor, advocate, and consultant since 2014—and he has made every possible mistake so you won't have to.

A graduate of Columbia University and a former Wall Street trader, Omid is an entrepreneur and a popular explainer of complicated financial topics. He has been interviewed by CNBC, Fox Business Network, the *Nation*, Slate, Minyanville, and *Handelsblatt*, the leading German-language daily. Best known for his viral videos and animations on YouTube, Omid's work has also appeared in the *New York Times*, the *Wall Street Journal*, Forbes.com, and the iTunes music store.

Other accomplishments include having his work tweeted by Tony Robbins, introducing the nickname "The Bernank" to the business vernacular, and being shafted by his record label for the $98.47 in royalties he is rightfully owed.

Acknowledgments

This book would not have been possible without the help of a team of professionals including my editor, Christina Verigan; designers Karen Minster and Laura Duffy; illustrator Simon Sullivan; and proofreader Debra Nichols.

I am also grateful to my close friends and family for being supportive and helpful throughout the writing process, especially Duda, Naz, Az, and Ji Young.

My thanks to Flavia for practically forcing me to make my first cryptocoin transaction.

Lastly, I want to thank all the tinkerers, thinkers, entrepreneurs, engineers, hackers, and hodlers who helped create this fantastic new world for me to write about. Blockchain technology is the greatest source of individual empowerment we have seen in a long time, but it never would have come about if not for a select group of people who were willing to question the status quo and imagine that there might be a better way.